BUILDING
RESILIENCE

HOW TO MOVE PAST FEAR INTO
REAL TOUGHNESS AS A TEAM

ROBERT TESCHNER, CHRIS STRICKLIN, LUKE LAYMAN

ROBERT GARLAND, BRIAN EMME

BUILDING RESILIENCE: How to Move Past Fear into Real Toughness as a Team

Copyright © 2023 by Chris Stricklin. All rights reserved

Cover images: © Pixaby
Cover design: Noel Sellon
Interior layout design: Jennifer Woodhead

Published by RTI Press
A VMax Group, LLC imprint, Chesterfield, Missouri, USA.

Library of Congress Cataloging-in-Publication Data:

Names: Teschner, Robert, author.
          Stricklin, Christopher, author.
          Layman, Luke, author.
          Garland, Robert, author.
          Emme, Brian, author.
Title: Building Resilience: How to Move Past Fear into Real Toughness as a Team
Description: First edition. | Chesterfield: RTI Press, 2023.
Identifiers: ISBN: 978-1-7329298-2-1
Subjects: LCSH: Leadership. | Teamwork. | Resilience. | Teams. | Organizational effectiveness.

Printed in the United States of America

10 9 8 7 6 5 4 3 2 1

PREFACE

What's increasingly apparent is that life, though amazing and full of incredible opportunities and goodness, is also rife with pain, disappointment, anguish, and despair. On the heels of several years dealing with the implications of a global pandemic, we are as a nation and society grappling with the exposure, deepening and widening the existing fractures within our various societies to such a degree that it feels like we're on two sides of a great divide. And it's a divide where the other side is wrong. "If you're not with me, you're against me" seems to be the underlying theme, coupled with very low empathy throughout the world.

Add to this the fact the media outlets suggest daily that things are getting worse and it's always someone else's fault. Never mind that we have a major land war in Europe for the first time in decades, a war which shows no sign of reaching any sort of resolution. Fuel prices are up, food prices are up, inflation is higher than it's been in decades, and it's harder to do the simple things than it was four years ago.

Gallup's CEO, Jon Clifton, recently published *Blind Spot*, a book about the global rise of unhappiness. In it, Jon outlines how the burden of dealing with never-ending disruption is affecting our collective souls. This is a difficult challenge to address, and it is an especially difficult time to lead. Authors of this book, we personally have been students of leadership since we were in our teens, and we collectively believe right now is the most difficult time in our lifetimes to be called to lead anything or anyone.

So where do we go to find hope in a better tomorrow, regardless of what today had in store for us? Where do we go to find a strategy, a roadmap for persevering even as everything continues to fall apart? Where do we go to find inspiration? To pick ourselves up after a loss, to find a way forward even as our strength begins to wane?

Our simple answer: *We turn to those who lived this approach all their professional lives.*

It just so happens that members of the military, and specifically members of high-performance, front-line military teams, have had to figure out a way to keep hope for a better tomorrow even as 'today' fell apart at the seams. They not only traced a roadmap through uncertainty and disruption but were then able to live it and teach it, equipping a new generation of warriors do the same. It so happens that members of front-line combat teams have had to find a way to bounce back from loss, reform, then learn and return to battle to win the war.

And it so happens we have five such team members who have agreed to share what they've lived and what they've learned in this book to help you.

It is the aim of every book in this series—the Military Mentorship Mastermind Series—to be read during a normal, nothing special, non-stop flight somewhere in the world. Our intent is to make our content digestible and practicable in the form of a very short and easy read. Every chapter can be consumed as a stand-alone event, and each ends with Points to Ponder. Our Points to Ponder (or PTPs) serve as guidance for your reflections and are designed to help you take action on and implement what the various authors propose. And, when you're ready, we have more resources available for you at www.MilitaryMentorshipMastermind.com.

Most importantly, please know **each of our authors wrote this book for YOU**. You were on our minds as we wrote our chapters. It's your ability to lead and care for your people confidently, with enthusiasm and vigor, even amid nonstop pain points and disruptions, that focused our writing and caused us to share, with incredible vulnerability, our personal and professional experiences.

And some of us have never before shared what we're sharing with you in this book...

"Why," you might ask, "did you write this for me?" Simply because our world desperately needs capable leaders, solid leaders, steady leaders, accountable leaders, inspirational leaders, vulnerable leaders—our world needs *real leadership* **now more than ever before in our lifetimes**. We want to help you to be who the world needs you to be, and a huge part of your leadership ability is dependent on building your resilience.

So, let's get to work. Let's start *Building Resilience*!

Some wake up to an alarm.

Others wake to a calling.

Find Your Calling!

CONTENTS

CHAPTER 1

WHAT
HAPPENS
TO US

M any believe life is what happens to them. What happens to a person is not the whole story, only the beginning. The influencers in the Military Mentorship Mastermind know that who we are is defined in how we react and grow through the experiences of life. Many also believe resiliency is the ability to endure traumatic experiences. Again, not entirely the truth. Mere endurance of life's experiences is not true resilience, only the effect. For the Military Mentorship Mastermind resilience means growing through our experiences; not merely enduring the pain, but blossoming from it. This deliberate focus on continual growth propels us beyond the ability to tolerate a trauma and utilizes the capability and capacity to emerge a stronger person and a higher performing team on the other side of challenge. For us, each challenge in life is a chance to learn, to grow, and to improve. For us, each stumble, each trip and fall is a chance to stand back up stronger and taller than before. For us, our story gets better through every success, achievement, trauma, and challenge.

In the pages that follow, our select group of authors, each with their own compelling stories, will address our most challenging moments in life. Our focus is on building resilience, and the path demands that we begin with vulnerability. Our collective experiences include cancer, aircraft crashes, combat weapons employment, and the death of a wingman. These are moments some of us have never shared before, moments in our lives we are detailing for our growth, for your growth, and to enable conversations revealing how we grew through them and owned the situations and the resulting effects on our lives, instead of merely enduring and allowing the situations to own us.

It is our shared belief that life is not what happens to you. Instead, life becomes what you make it as you intentionally grow through the moments that challenge you. While our present should be the culmination of the lessons learned in the past, our actions, inactions and reactions, our decisions, and indecisions, it too often is the result of passive learning in the form of situations experienced, instead of lessons learned, with no personal or process improvement made. Our goal is to empower you to grow from every interaction of every day and to refine and improve how we do the same.

This all-encompassing resilience does not happen naturally, or easily. In order to build resiliency, we must first embrace vulnerability. Our authors will discuss some of the darkest moments in their lives and careers to be deliberate about vulnerability as a foundational building block to inspire others to achieve success through building resiliency in their own lives.

This book was composed with you on our minds in every moment. We are military professionals; we serve others. We are instructors; we teach and train others what we have learned. This focus allows us a stated goal of making a difference. All the while, the act of authoring these stories and pages turned out to be critical to our own growth. While many experts, with letters such as PhD, MD, LCMHC, LPCC, and an alphabet of others, have purported to define resiliency, the authors of this manuscript do not display such designations. We merely display the badge of life experienced, hard-earned, and learned. Many of our experiences were not endured by choice—the traumas and the tragedies—but gratitude for the experiences and the growth found in each. Experience shapes the person we are today. These life lessons arm us with whole person knowledge of how to move forward in intentional growth. They also arm us with the why, what, and how to teach others and empower their growth. This book is written by five combat-proven senior military leaders turned business executives, each having lived through life-altering trauma. In no way do we think we have all the answers, but we are willing to devote time to becoming more tomorrow than we are today. We are willing to invest in others because we know that is how we truly grow ourselves.

To better understand the different results from trauma, let us examine a story told throughout the ages of a set of twins. For the purposes of this examination, only one aspect of their upbringing is important. They were born to an alcoholic father. Fast-forward to their thirties, and the two siblings, raised in the same environment, could not have matured and achieved in more different manners. One is just like his father: has pushed away all those who love him, scrambles from job to job, barely making it by in life. He ends every day with a fade into an alcoholic fog. When asked why he chose this path in life, he bellows, "Because of my father. I live from his example." He continues his explanation as he details that he had no choice, destined to this alcoholic life from his similar upbringing, a simple victim of circumstance. He is merely surviving each sunrise to sunset in this world.

More important to our story is the other twin. He is thriving in life with a beautiful family, a loving wife, and enjoying success in every undertaking. When asked how he paved this path in life, he proudly proclaims, "Because of my father. I live from his example." His pride flows with an explanation of how his father, in the good times, demonstrated the love and caring of a good family. He demonstrated how to be a father worth emulating. As his father's demeaner changed in later times with alcoholism, he demonstrated how not to live, how not to love, how not to be a father, how to allow tragedy and hardship to dominate your life into one of merely surviving, not thriving. The twin concludes with the simple sentiment, "I would not be the man I am today if not for the man my father was then. We are not what happens to us unless we allow that to be the story. We must use every experience, both the successes and the challenges, the tears of joy and the tears of anguish, to empower a better tomorrow than today. It is up to each of us to decide, do we accept being a victim, or are we determined to emerge a victor?"

In a similar manner, we ask you to join us on our life journey. We will share intimate and personal examples of trauma that continues to empower each of us to grow. From aircraft ejection to combat flights and a cancer diagnosis—with each challenge our group embraced every second, determined to stand strong through the trials and tribulations to emerge even stronger the next day, better prepared for tomorrow and whatever the future may hold.

It is our hope that these simple pages will serve as the seed to grow your tree of success stronger than it is today and inspire others to do the same. The strength of any tree is found in the roots, hidden beneath the surface. Resiliency is the roots of our tree, feeding our success and crucial to withstanding strong winds, heavy rains, and environmental stresses. The trunk of our tree is the main structural support, formed by our beliefs, attitude, habits, experiences, and values. As we look to the branches of our tree, we envision our team, our mentors, our confidants, and our relationships. The purpose of the branches is to reduce stress on the trunk and roots, and that is exactly what deliberate connections and meaningful relationships enable.

Our dedication in every aspect of life is continuous improvement. Our quest is for something we can never achieve: perfection. While we know perfection is likely impossible, it is the pursuit of perfection that ensures we get closer each day to achieving it, learning from challenges faced. Perfection is about the result, while excellence is about the process by which we perform. Resilience is key to our performance to enable growth. Our influencers on this team align on one quote above others to guide resilience, one penned by President Roosevelt in 1910, commonly known as "The Man in the Arena":

> *It is not the critic who counts; not the man who points out how the strong man stumbles, or where the doer of deeds could have done them better. The credit belongs to the man who is actually in the arena, whose face is marred by dust and sweat and blood; who strives valiantly; who errs, who comes short again and again, because there is no effort without error and shortcoming; but who does actually strive to do the deeds; who knows great enthusiasms, the great devotions; who spends himself in a worthy cause; who at the best knows in the end*

the triumph of high achievement, and who at the worst, if he fails, at least fails while daring greatly, so that his place shall never be with those cold and timid souls who neither know victory nor defeat.

As you ponder the following pages, remember values lie at the heart of our stories and culminate in a family, one not connected in name but in mission, belief, passion, purpose, and dedication. It is our quest to be better tomorrow than we were today and to help others achieve self-actualization while we are on the journey to reach our true potential. Together we can achieve more than we ever dreamed individually! Do you accept the challenge to reach for your true potential?

POINTS TO PONDER

1.1.　Start a journal. To truly embrace the challenge to reach our highest protentional is a journey of deliberate growth. We find it beneficial to journal our thoughts and lessons learned and pen motivational quotes and nuggets of wisdom from our mentors. Start a journal, one that is dedicated to your growth on the journey of life. Keep it with you all the time, close at hand when a brilliant idea arrives, or a lesson is learned.

1.2.　Who is your Peer 5? We believe you are the average of the five people you spend the most time with. Who are yours? You should be able to promptly name your five at any given time, and it should be a list that when said out loud, others that know you well would acknowledge their agreement.

1.3.　What is your focus? Understand your focus for this year and visit it often. This will lead you to a focus for this month, this week, this day, and every interaction.

CHAPTER 2

BUILDING THE WARRIOR MINDSET

Perspective & Insight of
Robert 'Cujo' Teschner

L ife is full of pain points. Call them disruptions, call them hits, call them failures, call them whatever you want. Bad stuff (along with a lot of good) is always coming our collective way. From the new car tire hitting a nail and deflating right after installation to the excruciating loss of someone we love, life is abundant with sadness, with troubles, with pain. Dad always said, "Life ain't easy," and he was right. In fact, to achieve anything meaningful in this life, the path to success is paved with pain. And to anyone who says, "Once we get past this problem, we'll be in smooth waters," I'm sorry to disappoint. Life will always be disruptive. *HOW WE DEAL with disruptions is what matters.* The mindset we adopt in preparing for and approaching each disruption will determine how well we make it through the pain. Warriors know how to prepare for, approach, and grow through disruption. Adopting the "Warrior Mindset" should be the ambition of anyone who wants to succeed in a sea of turbulence and challenges.

You might be asking, "What is the Warrior Mindset?" To me, and this is very much my view, the Warrior Mindset is an overall and all-encompassing approach to life that suggests to us, "When things get bad—when they get really painful, regardless whether it's in a figurative or literal way—*our story just got better*."

It's this mindset that guides us through turbulence, one that affirms while we know things are going to be tough and at times feel unfair, we're going to find a way forward and eventually shine because of it. It's a mindset that reminds us to consider in the midst of disruption and pain how much better the story we'll tell will be after we come through it successfully.

Upon reflection it turns out I had a predisposition to this way of thinking as a young man. By way of example, I recall the agony of being denied acceptance into the United States Air Force Academy. Attending the Academy was a primary ambition of mine since I was young. I was banking on making it in; acceptance was a necessary step in my plan to achieve my overarching dream of becoming an Air Force fighter pilot.

In an instant, my dreams were crushed, and my future was uncertain. A one-page letter informed me that I not only didn't make it in, but I also wasn't even asked to try again the following year.

Where was my mind amid this devastating, dream-crushing pain? I distinctly remember looking up from that letter and telling myself, "If I'm going to fly fighter aircraft—my life's ambition—I've got to find another way." I moved quickly to fix my problem and committed to earning a pilot slot through Reserve Officers' Training Corps. Critically, in a moment of pain, I affirmed that I was going to battle on and achieve my primary objective. I resolved that nothing was going to stop me, and I was mostly at peace. In the heat of the moment, at a major pain point, I had a component of the Warrior Mindset; specifically, I wasn't going to become a victim.

Why didn't I accept victimhood in this difficult time? I have my suspicions, but no certainty. Maybe it was my parents' examples. Perhaps it was something in my genes. What I know for sure is that I was absolutely unwilling to accept a bad outcome as my final verdict. What I also realized in that moment was how satisfying it was to immediately move to a Plan B. I still had my objective in mind; I was simply going to achieve it another way. This purpose drove me and kept me energized. I firmly believe this was an important component in my ability to achieve resilience.

In a stunning and completely unexpected twist, several weeks after receiving my rejection letter I was accepted into the Academy. I attended and ended up doing well in my studies. Ultimately, I earned the pilot slot I so longed for. And after two years of rigorous training, I finally arrived at my first operational fighter squadron. I had achieved my dream. I was flying F-15s!

What I learned from the outset of my time in an operational F-15C squadron was that we were navigating disruption daily. From maintenance issues, like an engine's afterburner not lighting on takeoff and a radar not working properly in flight, to losing a team member to a simulated surface-to-air or air-to-air missile attack in the middle of the mission, to someone experiencing a major aircraft malfunction in flight and being forced to return home early, seemingly nothing ever went according to plan. Success in a fighter squadron meant learning to deal with nonstop disruption, nonstop tactical pain.

What really amazed me about that life—what was literally reinforced on a daily basis—was that *we were determined to win no matter what*. And when we won, the story we got to tell about the mission became so much better!

Make no mistake; fighter pilots take winning seriously. In our planning sessions, we planned for things to go poorly. We then devised ways to deal with the challenges we anticipated. In our pre-mission briefings, we literally told the story of what it would look like, sound like, and feel like when things went poorly. Then we outlined how we would overcome and win regardless. As we flew the mission and executed our plans, we then dealt with the myriad of disruptions in real-time. It turns out there is no pause button in flight. Pilots have to keep moving forward, for that is the only option. Then, after a week of physically demanding high-speed, high-stress flights, we assembled as a group on Friday afternoons in the squadron bar for a ritual we called "Roll Call".

"Roll Call" was an event I used to live for as a young fighter pilot. It is one of the most important, and in my opinion one of the most fun, tribal rituals in a fighter squadron. It's one that takes place in the squadron bar. The atmosphere is festive, and the point is to celebrate making it through another challenging week in a dangerous business. A huge part of the celebration involves telling stories about what happened throughout the week. Not surprisingly, the best stories aren't about how everything went according to plan. The best stories are the ones where everything fell apart from the get-go and yet we still found a way to win. Sharing how we learned to adapt and overcome, how we were able to flex and react and truly dominate, those were stories worth listening to and telling!

Growing up in a squadron environment, where the expectation was clearly, "We're going to win despite anything that happens," quickly makes an impact. This dominance mindset, centered around a warrior ethos, is contagious and becomes part of both our collective and individual DNA. It shapes the way we think and approach problems. It affects how we talk about disruptions. It guides how we act and react. We begin to measure performance not based on how many things go well, but rather on how well we adapt in the moment and overcome when everything goes to hell.

What's fascinating is that everyone on the team adopts this mentality. I might have personally had a predisposition to it, but in the fighter squadron, there isn't a choice. A new fighter pilot embraces the Warrior Mindset, or they find themself out of a job. In the fighter pilot business, we don't make room for victimhood. We also have no patience for people who whine.

Like my teammates, I fully embraced the Warrior Mindset. I understood it as "the fighter pilot way." I didn't question the approach, I embraced it. I loved (and still do) the fighter pilot ethos, the warrior spirit, and the shared ambition to win at all costs. I felt incredibly fortunate to be part of a team that lived and breathed this ethos in all we did. I even felt bad for those who didn't know and live this way in their work. This ethos became my norm. *It became the only way to look at the world.*

And then life reared its ugly head again and put me to the test. This time around, it wasn't a case of being rejected from a school. It wasn't having to overcome a technical issue or the loss of a wingman during a difficult mission. It was much more personal this time around.

On the heels of my first-ever colonoscopy, my doctor informed me that he found a massive tumor in my lower colon. He also told me it would be five days until we received the biopsy results. In other words, we wouldn't know for at least five days whether I would have days, weeks, or months left to live. When I say 'we' I'm referring to my bride and myself—we were both sitting side by side as the doctor shared the news. All we knew in those initial moments was: *This is bad. The biopsy will tell us just how bad. We have to wait to get the results. And regardless, the forthcoming surgeries are going to be horrible.*

But what was my mindset in the midst of this horrible news? I clearly remember what I said to my bride as we sat across from each other in the little restaurant, shortly after leaving the doctor's office, each of us still stunned by the news he dropped on us like a bomb. I remember grabbing my bride's hands and looking her right into her eyes. I told her with absolute certainty one simple sentence:

"Diane, our story just got better."

What's amazing to me is that in that moment of confusion, uncertainty, sadness, fear, and pain, she both understood *and agreed.*

In that moment we both embraced a mindset that by this point was instinctive to me and was becoming instinctive to her.

Years later, I'm here to testify to the power of the approach. I'm still alive, and I'm here to advocate for the extreme necessity of having the right mindset going into battle. I'm a major proponent for having the right mindset to navigate the fear, the pain, the uncertainty, and the potential loss any given day might have in store for us. And I'm also advocating for being ready to keep moving forward regardless.

It just so happens that in our case, ***our story also and most definitely got better...***

POINTS TO PONDER

2.1. When disruption strikes, what is your natural response? Do you view it as something to be overcome in order to tell a better story? Is it something that sets you back, crushes you for a bit? Or something else, something in between? Why do you think this is your natural response?

2.2. What would you like your natural response to disruption and pain to be? What do you think it's going to take for you to get there, if you're not already where you want to be?

2.3. Imagine you just received some devastating news. Perhaps tens of thousands of dollars have just been stolen from your bank account. Maybe you just lost your biggest, most important client. Perhaps your #1 employee just tendered her notice. Pick something that would be a devastating loss to you. Imagine being in that moment. How do you behave and respond? Now, take a pause to reflect on how you would prefer to respond. Then visualize living in such a way that in the midst of pain and despair you will act in alignment with your best self. Now try to do this the next time you are actually confronted with this kind of a circumstance.

2.4.   Journal what you're thinking through here, keep-
         ing a record of those thoughts—a record you'll
         return to when you need them.

CHAPTER 3

IN THE HANDS OF GOD: THE CRASH OF RAPTOR 14

Perspective & Insight of
Robert 'Shark' Garland

One one-thousandth of a second...

A blink of an eye...

An amount of time which means nothing to most people.

An amount of time which means everything to my family.

A single millisecond was the time between sharing this
story and flowers on my tombstone.

t was a beautiful afternoon in Las Vegas, Nevada with crystal-clear skies and a gentle winter breeze. No other aircraft were flying at the time; it was as if the airfield was mine alone. "Raptor 1, you are cleared for takeoff." With this clearance from air traffic control, I pushed the throttles forward listening to the gentle hum of two Pratt & Whitney F119 Twin-Spool, Augmented Turbofan engines increasing power toward their 70,000 pounds of thrust.

The weight of the task at hand rested heavy on my shoulders: the first-ever test and evaluation of the Air Force F-22 Raptor. The year was 2004. I had the honor of being a member of an elite group of Fighter Pilots assigned to the 422nd Test and Evaluation Squadron. I was ready. One last performance check. All critical instruments in the green, and now a go for takeoff. Brakes release, the powerful machine surges forward with the acceleration of a top fuel dragster down the runway... 50 miles an hour, 100 miles an hour, 150 miles an hour. A gentle pull on the control stick and the anticipation of the graceful climb into the sky as I experienced countless times over my fourteen years of service.

Then, everything changed. Instead of a graceful lift off, the Raptor jumped into the air. *That's not normal*, I heard experience say in my inner monologue. The jet began to swerve in the air. Left, then right. Like skidding on an icy highway. Then the aircraft's nose violently rose skyward, not adhering to my commands. Training kicked in as I selected full afterburner to overcome the pending stall. The nose snapped back toward the ground faster than I thought possible. *Power back*! I fought the controls to keep the beast flying all the while thinking, *I've got this. This is why hours were spent in simulators and training.* My Air Force training took over, and I was driven by the mental model every pilot relies on in emergency situations:

1. Maintain aircraft control.

2. Analyze the situation and take appropriate action.

3. Land as soon as conditions permit.

My goal right then was simple, at least simply stated: safely fly away from the ground and check out the problem. My left hand instinctively moved forward to the landing gear handle. As the gear began retraction, the Raptor violently rolled right, a change from the previous swerving movements. Snap! Rolling upside down! *This is BAD!* Again, from instinct built through incredible Air Force training, my left hand transitioned from the landing gear handle to the ejection handle. In this moment, time stopped. I pushed back into the seat, whispered a gentle prayer, and pulled the ejection handle with all my might!

What happened next violates several laws of physics. Onlookers saw the mighty F-22 swerving in the air just above the runway, flipping end over end, and then impacting the Earth in an inferno of fire. Silence. Nothing. No parachute. No pilot. No ejection observed.

An ejection seat in a front-line, best-in-the-world fighter jet is a technical marvel. Many mini miracles must be executed flawlessly in order to give a pilot the chance to survive. The entire process from beginning to end takes approximately 1.25 seconds. When a pilot pulls the ejection handle, explosives and rockets in the canopy ignite to blast the canopy away from the cockpit. A rocket motor fires driving the seat up and out of the plane with the pilot sitting in it. When I pulled my ejection handle, there was a problem. Raptor 14 was rolling upside down and was completely inverted in 1.5 seconds. My ejection seat departed the plane at 92 degrees of right bank (I was technically upside down), approximately 100 feet in the air and moving nearly 210 miles per hour. The ejection system designers later said this ejection was clearly "outside the survivable ejection envelope."

An ejection is a violent experience. All pilots practice emergency procedures in ground simulators often. Once out of the plane and free from the ejection seat, an ejecting pilot transitions to an airborne skydiver... which is not something we practice. On what initially seemed a perfect day in December, I found myself unexpectedly skydiving. Now away from the aircraft, training still surged procedures through my mind, and action drove me to the post-ejection checklist: Canopy, Visor, Mask, Seat kit, 4-line, Steer, Prepare, Release. Step one is to confirm and analyze the parachute canopy. I looked up for the canopy, but nothing, no parachute...my heart sinks. *Not good.* No time to waste! I skipped straight to the end of the checklist and looked down at the ground. It was getting close really fast! *This is really bad!* Only feet above the ground, free-falling at 200 miles per hour, I braced for impact. *This is going to hurt.*

Back to the miracle… Imagine you are holding someone, and you gently lay them down on the ground. Like you would place a sleeping child on their side in their bed to not wake them. That is what happened to me. It was as if giant hands caught me and simply laid me on the ground. I did not skid, roll, or tumble. No damage, dirt, or debris from the desert runway on my uniform. My flight gear was spotless.

As I laid there, I watched the F-22 explode at the end of the runway in a massive ball of fire. Time slowed as I waited for the expected indescribable pain before the arrival of my death. Nothing. No pain. It was thirty-three seconds from brake release on takeoff to lying on the ground next to the runway. I stood up and began checking my survival gear—a habit from always using a checklist. As my eyes focused behind me, I saw what I had so longed to see before landing…my parachute. Only it was not fully deployed and blossomed from opening. Instead, it was connected to me with seventy-five feet of cord stretched out, lying in a straight line. Unopened. The stitching on my harness where the parachute risers connect still in place. The parachute did not have time to open.

A helicopter was practicing landings nearby. The pilots landed on the runway near where I was standing. While checking my survival gear, I noticed one of the pilots running toward me. "Dude, are you okay?" He asked in amazement. As he stood before me in awe, he handed me a piece of cloth and said, "This must be yours." What to many would be a simple cloth was to me a badge of honor. The cloth was my U.S. Air Force Weapons School Graduate patch, a sacred symbol of my chosen profession which had blown off during the ejection. My fellow serviceman had picked it up from the middle of the runway on his sprint over. His eyes widened in bewilderment as I calmly slapped it back on my left shoulder where it belonged.

After a brief trip to the hospital for a medical evaluation, my wife Amy arrived. Those who know our family know Amy is the pillar of our home. She is a Texan and a powerful woman of faith. She is compassionate, kind, and always first in line to serve others. After a good hug, Amy calmly said, "Well, you've had an interesting day."

"Yes, ma'am, we have." I gently responded.

We all know how truly important resilience is to success in life. Although none of us want to experience trauma, experiencing challenges is one of life's greatest teachers if you embrace the growth possible on the other side. The events above of 20 December 2004 will always remain a surreal experience, one I would never wish on anyone.

Fast-forward to three weeks after my brush with death. This was the true test of my personal resilience and character. There is an old saying, "When you get bucked off a horse, get right back on." The goal is to subvert paralyzing fear following a traumatic experience. The longer you wait to resume an activity when the trauma occurs, the harder it becomes. For me, that was absolutely true!

On 6 January, the squadron flying schedule placed me back into an F-22 for the first time after my surreal experience. The flight was a two-ship to continue F-22 tests, and I was the wingman. We all knew the mission's primary purpose was to get me back in the air, back in the saddle. On the taxi to the runway my Raptor had a maintenance failure preventing flight. During the entire taxi, I had been quietly praying for the plane to give me a reason not to fly. I had NO desire to face that takeoff experience again. NONE! With a sigh of relief, I said to myself, "Yes, it broke!" After aircraft shutdown, I drove home as fast as I could. I wanted NO part of this! Next day, next Raptor. On this day we took the runway for takeoff. My pulse surged, and my breathing stopped. Another problem, another excuse. After returning the Raptor to the parking spot, I ran inside the building...not my fault. But something else was wrong. I could see everyone staring, and I knew what they were thinking... I drove home.

If the previous two weeks weren't bad enough, I had to sleep on this challenge for the next three nights. Then Monday came. Monday, three weeks to the day since my ejection. The day looked the exact same...beautiful, clear sky, 3:30 in the afternoon, and I was alone, one jet, yet again. As the runway approached, prayers multiplied for this jet to give me a reason not to fly. If there is a mechanical problem preventing flight, it is the jet's problem, NOT mine! Nothing wrong with me.

As I took the runway for takeoff, my prayers intensified. The last chance before takeoff, I radioed the control tower, "Raptor 1, ready for takeoff." The tower controller called back, "Raptor 1, you are cleared for takeoff." My eyes trained on the runway in front of me. I saw something I had never experienced. A mountain—one of emotion, fear, adrenaline, and anxiety—an obstacle I immediately thought insurmountable. My very own Mount Everest. My hands began to shake, mouth went dry, and sweat poured into my eyes...I could hardly breathe. The last time I faced this runway, I survived by the blink of an eye. Time froze once again. Is this really worth it? What about my family? I'm supposed to be a husband to Amy. I'm supposed to be a father. Our daughter, Haley, was four years old and our son, Weston, was only 4 weeks old! Time must not have stopped, and I don't know how long I sat there on the end of the runway before my anxiety daydream ended. I never heard any other radio call from the tower controller asking, "Raptor 1, did you hear me? Are you okay?"

This moment will forever be frozen in my mind, in my psyche. It was like nothing I had ever experienced in life. It was the moment I learned something big, about myself, about my family, about life. In that moment, I truly felt why a resilient character matters. My thoughts were of my purpose, my values, my 'why' in life. In that moment there was only one choice...is this what you have been made to do or not?

My eyes instinctively surveyed the display instruments one more time, praying for something to break. All Green. Release brakes. The jet began the familiar surge of acceleration down the runway. Again, time slowed. The next few seconds were experienced in slow motion for me. The airspeed began to increase as I gently commanded the aircraft off the ground. The Raptor lifted gracefully into the air. As I reached for the landing gear handle, I closed one eye and held my breath. The wheels retracted without a hitch. My eyes focused down the runway, and I saw a grey silhouette of Raptor 14, still burned into the concrete from three weeks earlier.

In a mere second, the end of the runway approached. With a surge of adrenaline, I pulled back on the stick, the G-Load spiking at maximum. I slammed the throttles forward into full afterburner and rocketed straight up. The Raptor responded in kind as she thrust me skyward. I rotated in my seat to look back over my shoulder. The runway faded in the distance and the mountain, the one I felt insurmountable, dissolved into mist. Back in the saddle. Now time to SOAR into the rest of life.

We all respond to adversity and challenges in different ways. Lou Holtz, head coach for the Notre Dame football team, has shared many thoughts of wisdom. He once said, "Life is 10 percent what happens to you and 90 percent how you respond to it." Raptor 14 confirmed this to me. Why is personal and professional resiliency so important to high performance?

Everyone has God-given talents, skills, and abilities, sometimes referred to as our calling. By understanding and embracing our personal gifts and talents, we get a glimpse of what our calling may be. Our calling is our purpose in life. We all have a purpose. When we are living our purpose, we are best positioned to perform at the highest level of our potential. Both before and after that fateful Monday in December, I have known my purpose. For me, it is to be a man of strong faith first. Second, to support, care for, and lead my family. Third, to serve other people.

My time in life was not finished when Raptor 14 crashed. Rather, it was a new beginning. Why? It confirmed our family belief that tomorrow will be better than today. We understand personal resilience. It is a key to high performance both in our personal and professional life. The resilience template is simple. We work daily to live our purpose while building a home founded on love, faith, safety, and security. We ensure a positive balance between our own personal life and our work. We treat others with care, compassion, respect, and dignity. Finally, we always try to do the best job possible, no matter the task. This personal resilience builds confidence and commitment. It creates a sense of peace. It reinforces that we have a future, no matter the circumstance. My experience in Raptor 14 was life validating. Now, I have a story to show what a resilient life looks like. A story that proves the significance of believing why you are here and why it is important. Proof that we all have a purpose and a future.

POINTS TO PONDER

3.1. Do you know your calling? Are you aware of your personal talents, skills, and unique abilities? What are you great at doing? What comes naturally to you that others seem to work very hard to achieve? What do you love to do? Do you know what inspires you? Your answers define your calling.

3.2. If you are fortunate to be living your calling, what happens when disaster strikes? When everything you thought you were meant to do and be explodes? When your life appears to crash! Personal resiliency allows you to stand back and push forward. To be better tomorrow.

3.3. When life happens, what do you do to get back on the horse, get back in the saddle, and soar over that mountain of doubt, fear, and distrust? Where do you turn for guidance, for support, for a lifting hand? What are your personal resilient attributes?

CHAPTER 4

MINDSET AND APPROACH—
How We Mentally Practice Resilience

Perspective & Insight of
Luke 'PSYCH' Layman

As I talk to leaders around the world, there is a shared awareness of stress, but a lack of understanding of the types of stress and how to use it in your favor. Then there are the elite, those who have embodied the Warrior Mindset. They have a full awareness of stress and response, creating an elite level of resiliency that makes their armor quite impenetrable. The good news is the secrets aren't so secret, and by simply employing the skills in this book, you too can become superhuman.

Before entering a conversation about resilience, we must first discuss fear. F.E.A.R. can be defined as a Future Expectation of an Adverse Result, independent of its relative likelihood of occurrence. Where does fear come from? It comes from a threat perception, which then induces a stress response. But that fear must be correlated to a previously learned or lived experience.

A human baby does not fear a lion, nor does she fear a gun. As children, we become attuned to things that can do us harm. Our human disposition relies upon centuries of evolution that have stored data in our primitive brains to keep us safe. For example, our reptilian brain is designed to protect us from a lion attack. While the baby does not yet know she should fear the lion, her brain is actively working to keep her safe.

Resilience would be useless if not for stress and fear. If we are never placed under duress, we do not need resilience. Since you have most assuredly endured a significant amount of pressure before and will continue to endure stress in the future, you can learn how your body supports you in this stress response. Resilience is not fixed; it is elastic. It's not a matter of whether you have resilience or not; it's a matter of how strong your resilience is. The good news is that it can be trained like any other muscle.

As a warrior commits to battle, he knows there will be destruction and death. However, a Warrior Mindset does not involve being free of pain or discomfort, neither stress nor fear. Quite the opposite. The secret lies in his resilience. When faced with adversity, the elite measures how quickly he can return his body to a state of peak performance.

Fighter pilots commit to significant amounts of duress. We intentionally place our bodies and war machines between friendly forces and enemy combatants. Fear is both a constant and variable at the same time. I didn't have to be shot down to correlate fear to the threat of surface-to-air missiles. My job was to deliver precise weaponry on time and on target; fear was part of the job. In the A-10 Warthog, our weapon of choice was the 30-millimeter gatling gun, and our delivery of choice was a high-angle strafe.

My first time delivering a weapon in combat occurred in northeast Afghanistan amongst the Hindu Kush mountains that easily top 15,000 feet. From my position at 20,000 feet, I was only a few thousand feet above the mountaintop. As I located my target, I passed an attack brief to my wingman, instructing him to follow me in formation to employ a 100-round burst of his 30-millimeter gatling gun. I identified the target with an infrared pointer through my million-dollar targeting pod.

I radioed, "One's Tally", the code word for target identification.

My wingman responded, "Two's Tally."

We both gained a lock on our targets through our night vision goggles. Before tipping my wings, I experienced an overwhelming feeling of coldness. It was winter in Afghanistan, and the outside temperature was thirty degrees below zero. The inside of my cockpit, however, was slightly below

70 degrees. The coldness couldn't possibly be due to temperature. I was present to an increased level of stress and nervousness. Thoughts like, *What happens if I miss?* and *What if I kill a friendly?* raced through my head. I knew I had to beat back that doubt and be methodical with my decision-making. My brain snapped quickly to a technique used during air-to-air refueling to relieve stress and anxiety.

When flying in close formation to another airplane, pilots tend to 'ham fist' the airplane. Tightening our grip on the controls is a natural reaction to stress. The harder we squeeze, the more rigid our movements become. You can imagine the level of finesse needed when flying formation with an airplane the size of an airliner. The technique is simple: wiggle your fingers and toes. This technique was a trigger we used to overcome a subconscious reaction with a conscious stress reliever.

If I was feeling it, I felt confident my wingman was feeling it too. One last radio call: "Remember to wiggle your fingers and toes."

As I had done thousands of times before, I tipped my wings in the dark of night to point the nose of my A-10 Warthog to the target. I matched the weapons solution through my heads-up display with the infrared mark I saw through my night vision equipment. I squeezed the trigger and released a burst of 100 high-explosive incendiary rounds.

The weapons released from the airplane created a condition on the ground that was even more chaotic than before. Now the enemy knew I was there and had their sights set on a new target: ME.

After the attack run, I executed a Safe Escape Maneuver. With the airplane now passing 400 miles per hour and rapidly accelerating, I pulled back on the stick and jammed the throttle in a full forward position. I pulled the nose of the airplane through the horizon at seven times the force of gravity. I squeezed my abs as I felt my G-Suit inflate, reducing my risk of a G-Induced Loss of Consciousness.

Risking a loss of consciousness, the Safe Escape Maneuver is the fastest way out of the target area. I practiced this action hundreds of times before accomplishing one in combat. With each recovery, I conditioned my body to feel the G-Forces and created a coordinated response between body and mind that recovered the airplane to a wings-level condition at a safe altitude.

Years later, I learned that the cold sensation I experienced prior to rolling in was a stress response caused by a lack of circulation induced by a lack of oxygen. Despite six years of preparation for that moment, I endured what researchers refer to as an Acute Stress Response. Acute, in this application, does not mean *small*. It means *localized*, and it differs from chronic stress. It is imperative to note that acute stress comes with an intensity and a duration. Think of a wave in the ocean. The amplitude is measured from top to bottom, from trough to crest. The wavelength is the distance between the two waves. As stress appears, it is essential to note how tall the wave is and how quickly it passes.

There are two predominant groups of stress: acute and chronic. Your body naturally maintains a state of homeostasis, or a tendency to create a relatively stable equilibrium, between interdependent elements. The good news is that your body is constantly working to develop this balance. By practicing resilience-building behaviors, we make a new level of homeostasis. Imagine the difference in pain tolerance between a newborn and a holocaust survivor.

We often associate acute stress with high-stress activities or traumatic events. In practicality, it is actually much less pronounced. It can be as subtle as a change to your routine or an unexpected delay that disrupts the expectations of your day.

During my first weapons employment, I was experiencing the effects of acute stress, though I didn't recognize it as such at the time. Many of the stressors were overt. I knew consciously there were people on the ground with real weapons. But many of the stressors were much more covert—they were the forces at play in my subconscious. My body knew I was in a threatening environment, and my brain was working to keep me safe like it was designed to do.

Stress has a variety of signs and symptoms, including depression, anxiety, fatigue, difficulties with concentration and memory, hyperarousal, and social withdrawal. The pressure I felt in the cockpit is no different from any stress response you have felt. It could be caused by natural disasters, car accidents, the sudden death of a loved one, or receiving a life-threatening diagnosis.

Think of an acute stress response as a reaction to something you didn't expect. It's localized and short-term, but it still has an incredible impact.

To understand the Warrior Mindset, we take note of our human condition and response to stress. Imagine stress is like a bucket with a tap in the bottom. Stressors go in the top like water, filling the bucket toward its brim. The spigot on the bottom controls the release of stress. Later we will cover how to keep the bucket at equilibrium by managing what goes in and what goes out. Every human response is positively intended. The connection between your brain and body responses is designed to keep you safe.

Stress releases three hormones that energize your fight-or-flight response: cortisol, adrenaline, and norepinephrine. Across our human evolution, these hormones were designed to make us aware of the proverbial bear and give us the energy to fend it off.

Cortisol, the primary stress hormone, increases sugars (glucose) in the bloodstream, enhances your brain's use of glucose, and increases the availability of substances that repair tissues. Cortisol also curbs functions that would be nonessential or harmful in a fight-or-flight situation.

Adrenaline triggers the body's fight-or-flight response. This reaction causes air passages to dilate to provide the muscles with the oxygen they need to fight the danger or flee. Adrenaline also triggers the blood vessels to contract to redirect blood toward major muscle groups, including the heart and lungs.

As a neurotransmitter in the central nervous system, norepinephrine increases alertness, arousal, and reaction time.

Norepinephrine has been shown to play a role in a person's mood and ability to concentrate.

If acute stress is localized, chronic stress is persistent. High-pressure jobs or financial difficulties can cause it. It can also be caused by challenging relationships or an injury that prevents normal activities. It represents the baseline for the level of stress you have in your life. If we think about that same wave, chronic stress is the depth of the water. It's the difference between knee-deep, chest-deep, or in over your head.

In the example of the watering pail, chronic stress is the amount of water that stays in the bucket all the time. Therefore, cumulative stress is the sum of your acute and chronic stress. In combat, the chronic stress would be the constant threat of missile attack, and the acute stress would be an attack run or weapons employment.

In your daily life, cumulative stress may be associated with a challenging work environment, young children, aging parents, or health issues. When combined with an explicitly challenging acute stressor, your cumulative stress may reach a boiling point. This could happen through a car wreck, getting fired, or a bout with the flu.

If a stressor is persistent, or your stress bucket is at its brim, the body's resources will deplete. Chronic stress causes increased stress hormones and keeps your stress response constantly engaged, leading to fatigue. This is when burnout occurs.

To become more resilient, you must find your own Safe Escape Maneuver. When you know the mechanics of the maneuver, you practice until it becomes a habit. Our goal with this book is to give you the tools to adopt the Warrior Mindset in your own life. In your pursuit of mastery, you will lead others to become more resilient as well.

POINTS TO PONDER

4.1. Take an inventory of your current stress levels. On a scale of 1-10, how much cumulative stress do you currently have?

4.2. When thinking about past successes, what is your Safe Escape Maneuver? Specifically, look for the behaviors and characteristics that allow you to bounce back quickly from adversity.

4.3. What acute stresses have you experienced? What chronic stress do you carry? List them.

CHAPTER 5

AVOIDING THE BREAKING POINT

Perspective & Insight of
Brian 'Stickit' Emme

R esilience requires both rigidity and flexibility. It is like a tree branch. The branch bends and twists while holding firm to the base. If strong enough, it does not break when moved by a gust of wind, the weight of a bird, or any other event that causes it to displace. Resilience in nature for the mighty oak tree begins when it is a mere acorn. For humans, resilience is a learned trait that doesn't come naturally. For high performance teams, it is a required skill developed through learned behavior and training. For the oak tree, resilience is in its nature, for humans it is in our nurture. Nature over centuries of genetic evolution passes lessons via seeds. Teaching and learning are how humans pass along information. In high performance teams, we train each other to bend but not break. Training develops an individual's skills to collaboratively enable a team to perform at an elevated level.

My resilience nurture began early in my flying career. The flight was in an F/A-18 in Iraq during the opening weeks of Operation Iraqi Freedom. We were operating from the Mediterranean Sea, in the vicinity of Cyprus, 800 miles away from our targets. Each day we had to navigate through Turkey to avoid Syria to the south, then fly into the northern cities of Irbil, Mosul, and Kirkuk. The weather was terrible, as clouds and storms abounded. The snowcapped peaks rose into and hid behind the clouds. Our radar altimeters would often sound off as we flew over a peak we couldn't see. It was unnerving.

I was 'Dash 2' on a two-aircraft flight. We performed an armed reconnaissance mission, looking for enemy combatants, infrastructure, and equipment. We each were fully loaded with air to ground weapons and fuel. We were searching our Forward Looking Infra-Red (FLIR) targeting pods for signs of activity. The myriad of sensors required every ounce of concentration while still flying my aircraft. Then my priority shifted to a warning light illuminated in the cockpit.

The light indicated one of my Auxiliary Mounted Accessory Drives (AMAD) had lost oil pressure. It is one of the most important parts of this intricate machine. Immediately, I applied the appropriate emergency procedures. Step one, throttle to idle. My flight lead began making necessary radio calls to alert our teammates of the issue. The F/A-18 has two engines and can fly with only one. Operating the engine with an AMAD pressure failure can create conditions for a fire. This new reality changed our mission. We now focused our efforts on getting back to the ship safely.

The situation devolved rapidly. I now was in a heavily loaded single engine jet unable to perform air to air refueling over high mountains in terrible weather. Leadership on the ship wanted us to return if possible. I did not think I could make that happen safely. We have a saying in Naval Aviation: *If there is any doubt, there is no doubt.* If you aren't 100% sure you can accomplish a task safely, then it's time to make the decision to pivot. Rather than push a dangerous situation, you must weigh all your alternate options and choose a new course of action.

Returning to the ship was now out of the question. That left only two viable diverts in Turkey. The primary divert was well known and highly preferable, but it was high risk to reach. The second was within reach, but nobody knew anything about it: Diyarbakir. With fuel getting low, a decision was needed: take further risk to reach a better airfield, or accept the closer but unknown quantity? The flight lead's jet couldn't be taken out of the fight just to maintain section integrity. The choice was mine and became vividly clear after drawing on a Naval Aviation axiom: *if there is any doubt, there is no doubt.* It's time to divert alone into the unknown of Diyarbakir! The last radio call my friend and flight lead made to me as I detached with the field in sight: "Good luck!"

I landed hard. I heard the jet grunt as it settled its weight onto the runway. In broken and surprised English, the Turkish tower controller told me where to park. As I taxied into my parking spot, I could see a line of olive drab green military trucks racing in my direction. Some had lights flashing. My survival, evasion, and resistance training came to mind as I wondered what kind of reception I was to meet. Soldiers soon surrounded my jet. Some with rifles at the ready, others slung over their shoulders, trucks parked all around my jet. The engines were still turning, and my missiles were still armed. I frantically gestured for them to get away from my jet as these soldiers were wearing hats near my intakes. Hats can get sucked into the intakes and cause engine damage. I feared further injury to them or to my jet. So, I shut down everything before I could conduct my checklists. They were touching everything on it, including the weapons. They were shocked to see a US Navy fighter jet parked on their ramp with bombs and missiles on its wings. I was shocked I was now in Turkey!

I was the fourth most junior member of the squadron with a $60M dollar national asset, alone in a country not supportive of the US's involvement in Iraq. I would spend the next four days out of the fight considering my decision and the impact on our team. An intense sense of loneliness and regret would follow, as I knew tensions would arise because of the diplomatic clearance required for a rescue crew to come get me and the jet out of Turkey. But it was safe on deck, no further damage to the jet. We had bent, but not broken to avoid a worse situation, an ejection over a foreign country or in the ocean.

I managed to get in contact with my command on the ship the following day. The Commanding Officer was glad the jet was safe on deck, and I could tell he was working hard to get it recovered. The team would have to rally around this new reality of having one less jet in the mix to fight the war. He could tell I was frustrated to be out of the fight and concerned I had made a decision that put him in that bind. He told me to sit tight, he had it covered.

The beautiful thing about a high-performance team is how they react. True teammates rally around and cover for the decisions and actions of one of its members. I would be doing the same thing for my wingman if it were him or her in Turkey, just as they were doing for me. There was no second-guessing my decision. There was no shaming, no blaming, no guilt applied. It was a demanding situation. I made a decision informed by the reality of what was possible and not possible. My decision as the 4th most junior member of the squadron affected the team's ability to perform the mission. Yet as the aircraft commander for my jet, a single-piloted airplane, it was solely mine to make. I was responsible for the outcome.

We received training as junior aviators from the more senior pilots in the squadron about how to handle stressful situations. We learned how to analyze and mitigate risk. This training contributed greatly to the decision I was able to make in a stressful and deteriorating situation. The conservative risk mitigation concept of "if there is any doubt, there is no doubt" played in my head at the exact time I needed that guidance. I was able to rapidly make and accept the decision to divert into the unknown. "To live to fight another day" and "discretion is the better part of valor" are two similar idioms that convey similar guidance in deciding under arduous conditions to prevent making a situation worse.

Like the tree, whose seed develops its branches to bend and not break, so too can individuals learn to apply this concept. If the high-performance team's ecosystem teaches its youngest members these concepts, allows and empowers them to make decisions, and then supports them after they do, is it still a question of how or why American fighter pilots routinely carry out the mission despite setback? The individual and collective resilience of these organizations is possible because it is taught. Time is dedicated, even in busy schedules, to develop people who know how to make good decisions. The possibility of making sound decisions converts to reality by intentionally investing in our teammates' training. Teach them how to do it. Leaders then need to support those decisions. This method reinforces the potential that good decisions under difficult situations can be made—and made repeatedly. We don't magically rise to any challenge under stress, we simply default to the highest level of our training.

POINTS TO PONDER

5.1. How did you learn to be resilient? Who taught you?

5.2. Who do you have in your life who could teach you about resilience?

5.3. Who do you mentor in your life about resilience? In your family? In your workspace? Do you share your challenging experiences with others with the goal of helping them?

CHAPTER 6

THE FOURTH QUESTION OF TRAUMA

*Perspective & Insight of
Chris 'Elroy' Stricklin*

A challenge lay before us each and every day. A choice of how to deal with each day, each event. When faced with challenges, hurdles, and difficulties, will you become a victim or emerge a victor? The question is, as you live through these traumatic moments, do you merely survive, or are you dedicated and determined to accept the challenge to thrive?

Resilience is a pillar on which members of our military stand strong. Our way of life demands resilience as we move our families around the world at breakneck pace to meet the needs of our nation. Resiliency becomes a skillset we depend upon as we face battles with our nation's enemies through the fog and friction of war while protecting our way of life. The challenge continues when the smoke clears and the pace begins to slow. Many of us fear the unknown, the inevitable emergence of 'what now' and 'what next.'

Many define resilience simply as a capacity to both withstand and recover from difficulties. On this I disagree. The resilience commonly demonstrated in military members is not that simple. We do not desire to withstand and recover, instead we hunger to learn and grow. Ours is not the journey of enduring pain; it is one of advancing through it and becoming better on the other side. These words are not easy to write. For years I did not live them and could not speak to them. My focus was on enduring and surviving, not on recovering—and far from growing and improving as a result.

In the Fall of 2013, I wrote:

I do not dream. Sleep is darkness, a blank space bridging one day to the next. I hear people talk about their nighttime dreams, but none come to me. Is this normal? I remember a time when I dreamed. When past daytime experiences bridged to a vision of future adventures. How do you explain this to anyone? Who do you ask why?

I have never published or even shared these words until now. The time is now because the answer to these questions is now clear to me. I've realized my body was more resilient than my mind or emotions, protecting me from experiences I was not prepared to face. In the years since penning those words in my journal, I have relaxed the walls that protect my inner self. Vulnerability is a new strength I proudly display and use to encourage others to do the same. It has made room for growth and peace in my life, more than I ever thought possible.

As a fighter pilot and former Air Force Thunderbird, people often ask me, "Is there anything you are afraid of with all you have experienced?" The question has never been truthfully answered. If I had, the honest truth would have revealed the answer is: silence. After years of jet noise, most pilots have severe ringing in our ears, or Tinnitus, for which there is no cure. Again, a simple (and real) deflection on why we don't like silence.

The full truth rests in the reality of being resilient. Not the part where we endured the trials and tribulations of our life, but the challenge we embrace afterward to grow and improve from them. For me, it's the reality I faced once I realized I was not bulletproof and that a fighter pilot has feelings, ones which reveal vulnerability and forced me to look to my wingman for support. This vulnerability is not one reflected in young fighter pilots or a character embraced in the bravado of our fighter pilot culture, yet it is one each of us needs to develop. The reality is found in our experiences, challenges, and traumas of yesterday which hide in the shadows of our life and seem to catch up to us in silence.

For me, this came thirteen years after I survived what many experts deemed an unsurvivable ejection, thirteen years after my wife heard via phone call I had perished. On 14 September 2003, the majestic red, white, and blue Thunderbird F-16 I was piloting impacted the ground after a 25.25 second flight time, in front of approximately 85,000 spectators. My commander ordered Thunderbird 8 to call to my wife before pictures hit the news and before he had fully confirmed whether I had survived. She heard what every spouse dreads with all their heart, that her high school sweetheart, her husband, the father of her children, her best friend...had perished.

Being moments from death amidst an ejection isn't something I own uniquely—not even in this book. People always profess how resilient we are after these jolting escapes. That was not true of me, at least in the beginning. It was also not the *ah-ha* moment of my life when the smoke magically cleared and I emerged with mission and purpose. The months and years after my survival were more difficult and painful than the 40+G ride in the ejection sequence itself.

From the outside though, that was not the vision built. My wife and I hid the pain and struggle from everyone, even ourselves. Resilience is not merely facing the tomorrow you almost lost after surviving a trauma. That is pure survival. Resilience is being better tomorrow than you are today and utilizing the experience of the trauma as an empowering force from which to grow and thrive. It is learning through knowing yourself and truly being honest about your fears, short-comings, and strengths. It requires aligning with your 'why' in life—the north star which guides each action, inaction, and reaction, every decision and indecision—which provides structure and accountability for living.

Surround yourself with peers who challenge you to be more, to be truly better. These key individuals encourage you to live and grow supported by a safety net of vertical and horizontal mentorship that enables you to stand on the shoulders of giants, encompassed by those who have endured the challenge before, embraced by peers who are enduring similar challenges at the same time, and empowering the next generation to follow in your footsteps.

Finally, it is time to discuss the real drivers of resilience. Across the years, as I have sat with so many who survived so much, we all focused on the same three questions:

Why did this happen?

Why did this happen now?

Why did this happen to me?

These questions are common after trauma, and each of us can get more lost in one than the others. We drive ourselves into dark spaces searching for answers we may never find. These questions are the ones on which I focused in order to withstand and endure my experiences. But more important than those, the fourth question I now offer to trauma survivors, the question that drives the resilience mindset, is this: "Why did I survive?"

A focus on these four simple words will drive an awakening, letting the sunlight back into a survivor's life and paving the road to a better tomorrow. It is not in silence we find discomfort, but concern the shadow we cast, composed of past experiences following us in life, will catch us and force an inner reconciliation before we are ready. In this moment, we must look to the strategic offensive of war to guide our actions: the best defense is a good offense.

As we grow together through this work, we must realize our today is the result of experiences, decisions, actions, reactions, and inactions of yesterday. Both the good times and the trying ones make us who we are. Tomorrow will be the product of today's values, vision, thoughts, goals, focus, and desires. This is not merely individual resilience required to grow from our experiences, both the positive and the negative. Instead, it translates across our sphere of influence and tugs at the foundations of leadership. Good leaders give good news; great leaders also have the hard conversations. The resiliency of our leadership reflects our inner processes and capabilities. The first step of leadership improvement is to change the only thing you truly control, yourself. John Maxwell reminds us, "Personal growth is the only guarantee tomorrow will be better." From this we deduce the first steps to improving our leadership, toward a more successful company, or for engendering better relationships and building a better tomorrow is to start with a look in the mirror.

It takes individual dedication to embrace, not fear, a situation. This is not unique to me. Look to this book as a snapshot. We are five combat proven leaders—similar in experience and training, connected by the fact each has experienced life altering trauma and emerged stronger as a result—driven to make our experience mean more, to uncomfortably show our vulnerability so others may learn and grow through our pain.

The challenge lay before each person, as each of us have experienced trauma in our lives. The question is, did you merely survive, or do you accept the challenge to thrive?

POINTS TO PONDER

6.1.   What is hidden in your shadow? What is stored in your trauma closet you have never fully dealt with or even openly discussed? What situation or event in your life do you need to be transparently honest with yourself about?

6.2.   As military professionals, we have dedicated our lives to the service of others. This concept can be used to unpack trauma we do not want to deal with in life. When we look at our experience and realize the impact it can have on others, it gives an impetus to lower our defensive walls and openly share our challenges. In helping others grow, we grow. We develop a community of survivors who trust one another and help one another in life. How can others learn from your life experiences?

6.3.   Do you have a community of safe, like-minded individuals that you can share openly with? If not, what kinds of people might you be looking for in order to create that for yourself and others?

CHAPTER 7

BUILDING THE TEAM RESILIENCE APPROACH

Perspective & Insight of
Robert 'Cujo' Teschner

O ne of the things that made life in the fighter squadron special, one of the things that makes the high-performance team world of fighter aviation so exciting, is that you're almost never alone. Reflecting back on my time in fighter squadrons, it becomes clear to me that I never succeeded by myself, and I also never failed alone. Even when I was up there screaming across the skies at just under twice the speed of sound, I was very much operating as part of a well-oiled machine. I was always operating as a part of a team.

And we "teamed" exceptionally well in the fighter pilot world. I would say that "teaming," practiced well, is very much a learned skill. Getting people to operate together as an integrated whole, applying tried and true principles that allow for teams to team correctly—is a special undertaking. It's also an important approach to *Building Resilience*. Going it alone is a very tough road to take when it comes to the topic of this book.

Resilience as a process is a concept practiced exceptionally well by high-performance teams. The reason these teams practice resilience as a process is driven by that which differentiates a high-performance team from a regular team. According to Jon Katzenbach and Doug Smith, researchers who have spent over 20 years studying teams and writing about what they've learned, a high-performance team is one in which the team's purposes are nobler, goals are more urgent, and team approaches are more powerful. On high-performance teams, team members learn interchangeable skills and share leadership. Most importantly, *the team's ethos is one where if one team member fails, the whole team does.* And it's because of this ethos that the high-performance team world has adopted a ritualized practice of debriefing.

So then, what is a debrief? Simply put, it's the place the team goes to learn, grow, bounce back, and make the next mission better than the previous one. Formally, a debrief is the constructive evaluation of the quality of the decisions and associated actions measured against the objectives the team set out to achieve. At its core, the debrief is a unique approach to accountability that celebrates wins and helps a team have conversations about difficult subjects in a positive way. Most importantly, it's the process high-performance teams use to help them rebound on the heels of a failure. What separates the debrief from other team approaches to learning is that it serves as a means of building trust on the heels of a failure. It also serves as a means of motivating the members of the team to want to come back and try again.

While many people think they understand the concept of debriefing, few outside of the high-performance team world have experienced a debrief done correctly. Let's briefly examine two examples of debriefing, one that actively destroyed any hope of resilience, and the other, a masterclass in how to execute this process the right way. The first example comes from the 1986 version of the movie *Top Gun*.

In the original *Top Gun*, we get one very brief insight into the ritualized practice of learning that takes place after every flying mission. In the one debrief shown in the film, where Charlie (the character leading the process) summarizes her analysis by saying, "The engagement was a victory, but I think we've shown it as an example of what not to do," we see an example of debriefing that poisons the team.

In this debrief, the pilot being debriefed won his engagement by ignoring procedures and flying by instinct. On the heels of winning his engagement, the character known as "Maverick"—a callsign he earned by flying his way and not according to protocol—is verbally punished for not flying in accordance with established procedure. The tone Charlie uses is accusatory. Her conclusions are decided prior to any detailed analysis. "What were you thinking here?" she asks with an accusatory tone. Charlie actively attacks her student and, in so doing, almost guarantees that Maverick not only won't change his behavior but will most likely repeat the same kind of performance out of sheer pride. Battle lines are quickly drawn, and the outcome is one that pits teacher against student, polarizing the team in the process. After Charlie moves on to analyze a "textbook approach" to winning, one of Maverick's fellow pilots leans over and whispers to him, "Gutsiest move I ever saw, man." This comment helps solidify in Maverick's mind that he just got a raw deal. Maverick leaves the debrief upset and more deeply entrenched in his own approach to flying. The debrief is a failure as a means of team learning.

This movie debrief might inspire us to examine our approaches to learning, and especially to learning on the heels of a failure.

I travel the world every week, spending time teaching CEOs and senior executives how to practice effective accountability and how to do what I call "Debrief to Win." What I consistently hear from many of these senior executives is that they typically only debrief on the heels of a failure. They also note that the majority of the time, a debrief of a failure will lead to some form of punishment, and someone or some group of people will be singled out for having led the team to the failure. Then we analyze how excited the team is to participate in these debriefs, and the answer is that enthusiasm across the board is low.

Why is this? Why do we often treat a failure in a way that suggests that those who failed are bad people trying to do bad things to the organization? How does that approach help us to learn, to improve? And why, when left to our own devices, do we tend to gravitate toward criticism and the ability to find fault?

It's what I see and hear about all the time. And perhaps it happens because it's what we know.

In the end, we are products of the way we were raised. And in business, I've noticed that criticism, couched as "constructive criticism," is very much in vogue—it's almost a pandemic, and one that actively destroys the fabric of the team even as the original intent was centered on helping people improve. The term itself is an oxymoron…the term describes an internal conflict, one that can only serve to disappoint when applied. Then to this question: How does criticism affect resilience?

My answer is summarized in a very simple example: A woman I once met at a workshop told me that she stopped caring about her job months ago, specifically because the only feedback she ever received was "constructive criticism." She never heard about what she was doing correctly. She only heard about the things she was doing wrong. At some point, she stopped trying to bring her best. Instead, she started looking for another job.

Here's an alternative approach. Here's the way real high-performance teams harness the ritual of debriefing to learn, grow, bounce back, and to make the next mission better than the current one. To explain, I will use an example from my own experience learning in a fighter squadron.

Early in my career, I flew a mission where nothing went well. On the heels of this mission, I was extremely frustrated because we not only lost, but we lost badly. Everything that could have gone wrong did, and I was embarrassed, I was upset, I was disappointed, and I was angry—I was a mix of negative emotions, and it showed in the debrief. I took out my frustrations on my teammates, and my tone, attitude, and overall approach were absolutely deconstructive. I both felt and acted like a failure. It was a miserable experience.

Then I turned the debrief over to my instructor. It was his job to teach me and to help me learn from the experience. And what he did that day changed the way I led. It changed the way I thought about failure. It actually changed the whole approach I took to dissecting a loss.

My instructor said, "Brother, from my perspective, we were two decisions from victory today."

In one quick statement, he turned my world upside down. Not only did he inject positivity into what was a dark and emotionally charged experience for me, but he also shifted the approach we took to analyzing the disaster we had just flown together. Instead of highlighting all of the things we did poorly, he took a different approach. He was able to distill the mission down to the two key decisions that, had they been made differently, would have led to us coming away as winners. And in so doing, he was able to change my opinion of my own capabilities; he **inspired** me to want to go out there and try again.

And when I did try again, I won. My team and I won, largely because I believed in us again. And I believed because my instructor showed me that he believed in me.

As a result of my life's journey, I find I'm now a firm believer in teams.

I've lived an approach to teaming where resilience is boosted by way of a well-designed process for learning. If a debrief is the constructive evaluation of the quality of the decisions and associated actions measured against the objectives the team set out to achieve, then it's a means of team-learning from which every team member can benefit. Ultimately, I became the fighter pilot I was because of the power of the debrief. And on the heels of every failure, I was motivated to want to try again because I believed we would come back and win. May we focus on building resilience by, first of all, committing to building teams. And in learning to team well, may we create the foundation of resilience that allows us to be ready to bounce back every time we stumble.

POINTS TO PONDER

7.1. How well does your team "team?" If you were to rate your current team against others that you've been on, where does this one stack up? Why does it rank there?

7.2. Thinking back on the definition of a high-performance team, how close is yours to that definition? And how adept is your team with the understanding and practice of the ethos that says, "if one of us fails, we all do?"

7.3. In this chapter, we examined two versions of a debrief. Which one typifies the kind of debrief you're naturally inclined to deliver? Why are you pre-dispositioned to debrief this way? How about your teammates? What are their predispositions?

7.4. How prevalent is constructive criticism in your organization? What is constructive criticism doing to the culture you're building? How do your teammates respond to it?

7.5. You now have a very solid understanding of what a debrief is. What, if anything, was revealed to you as you thought on and pondered this definition? What, if anything, surprised you?

CHAPTER 8

ACCOUNTABILITY THROUGH TRAGEDY

Perspective & Insight of
Brian 'Stickit' Emme

Tragedy and mishap can happen to any of us at any time. We at Military Mentorship Mastermind understand it is not the event that determines who we are in this life; rather, it is how we respond, individually and collectively, that determines our level of resilience and true character. Resilience is not set at birth. It is a taught and learned behavior. It can be continuously improved. As leaders, in our lives and as part of our organizations, we control the quality of that response. Our decisions and actions improve the outcomes in our lives. These positive decisions impact our family and our organization.

All US Navy fighter squadrons deploy overseas on an aircraft carrier. Eight squadrons deploy as part of an air wing. Each squadron has specialized missions. The air wing is one of the most powerful tools in the strike group's arsenal. All squadrons attend Naval Air Station Fallon, Nevada as part of the readiness cycle. This is where air crews learn to fight. It was 'batter up' for us, our turn to train together at the highest level to be ready to deploy forward in combat. This was a routine training mission with the United States Navy. We would deploy to combat in six months.

The date was June 13, 2008. Then, two wars raged in the Middle East, one in Iraq and the other Afghanistan. This air wing while in Fallon knows it is going to combat. Stakes are always high for deploying forces to be good at our job. There is an added focus and incentive to be especially good when you know your destiny is combat. The Soldier, Sailor, Airman and Marine on the ground with a rifle in hand is expecting our best. Letting them down isn't on the table for discussion. Period.

We were ready to perform our air-to-air training mission that day, and so was our adversary. The 'merge' is the moment when two battling aircraft see each other and come together to finish the fight. Prior to this point they may only know of each other via their radar, or not at all. Once established in the visual arena to compete, it becomes a test: pilot versus pilot.

Only the better pilot will return home. This is a moment we simulate in training to prepare for combat. Adrenaline surges and focus sharpens. On this day, my wingman and I head to the merge with an adversary plane.

A training 'sortie' is our code word for a flight. I merged with the small black painted jet at 950 miles per hour of closure, 500 feet apart down my left side. I rolled 90 degrees angle of bank and pulled seven Gs across his tail to get behind him for a shot. I maneuvered 180 degrees of turn. My vision returned to full view from the tunnel vision the Gs had produced. I saw him in a right turn back toward my direction. I selected my AIM-9X Sidewinder missile and commanded the radar lock. With tone, I shot him in the face as he rolled out in my direction. I called my "kill" over the radio and focused on a safe second merge with the F-5 Tiger.

Following my second merge with the F-5, I looked over my right shoulder to see an enormous cloud of smoke. There were several vectors of flame, metal wreckage and shrapnel plummeting toward Earth. I saw the F-5 Tiger split into two halves aft of the cockpit. The tail appendage of the jet cracked and fell away engulfed in flame and smoke, spiraling out of focus. The front half of the jet with the cockpit continued forward and began to yaw. It started to spiral and spin out of control without wings to aid in its recovery. Two rapid smoke trails emanated from the cockpit. Each blossomed into a white and orange parachute canopy. They contrasted the sandy colored desert floor below. The massive hulk of metal hit the desert floor creating a mushroom cloud of dust, dirt, and fire. At 13,000 feet (about 3.96 km) over the desert floor, a mid-air collision between planes had occurred. Parachutes from one jet were visible, but not from the second. Training for that day was over.

In the literal blink of an eye, a young, motivated, energetic and smart Lieutenant had lost his life. His F/A-18 jet had collided with the F-5. His family and squadron-mates had to grasp the complex reality of his loss. Yet, the need to train and deploy remained. We had to replace those already forward. His family and our squadron would have to move forward. We had limited time to cope with the struggles of understanding and accepting his loss. Functioning in our new reality would be difficult.

The days, weeks and months immediately following the accident were a blur. We had a pause in the operational tempo and made a trip back to our home-station for the memorial ceremony. A missing man formation was flown over the church, a tradition of flying four planes in formation. In the moment just prior to overflying the ceremony, one jet selects full power and vertically leaves the formation to the heavens. The three remaining jets continue over the ceremony, with the space left open for our fallen comrade. It is a visual reminder of the gap, the loss, the hole in our hearts. That pause was brief and soon replaced by the requirements of the next evolution. The squadron remained on pace to continue its progress toward our goal. Despite the personal and collective suffering our team was facing, we had to move forward. As our path diverged from the family, we tried to focus on our jobs, as the family tried to focus on their new path. We stayed in constant touch though the distance and prioritization on our mission separated us. During a time when unity would be the best medication for the pain, we had to leave. Physical unity was not possible.

As the flight lead of that flight of two planes for that fateful day's mission, I accepted full responsibility. We are taught as flight leaders to take responsibility. Taught to not shirk responsibility for the safe execution of a scheduled mission. When a wingman is not brought home, there could only be one person held accountable: the flight lead. It was not easy, and I experienced dark moments when I assumed my squadron mates held me to blame. But nobody ever voiced that opinion. In fact, quite the opposite occurred. Because I had shouldered more than my fair share for that accident, the team rallied around me. The results of the accident investigation would later assign responsibility to three other members of the training event as contributory to the tragedy. It was not solely on me, according to them, but that didn't lessen the pain. The level of support I received from my team from the beginning was tremendous. My entire squadron was suffering and working through the tragedy together. My team's acceptance and support of me were the reason for the speed of my recovery. My resilience improved and allowed me to move forward. Without this support, it would have otherwise been a debilitating setback.

There is another time-honored tactic fighter pilots use to achieve laser-guided focus: compartmentalization. This is the term we use to describe the act of excluding from our minds any issues unrelated to our flights. Those issues are then put into a place for later. Compartmentalization allows us to focus on the task at hand, in theory, without distractions. It is an enormously powerful and effective tool when used properly. We use it to ensure we leave stressors, issues, emotions, and thoughts behind as we man-up our jets to perform complex missions.

I have found the power and value of compartmentalization. It is a means of ensuring localized, short-term mission success. It enables us to maximize safety. We cannot have life stressors on our minds at high airspeeds and narrow margins. As a matter of safety, it's imperative to remove those distractions from the cockpit.

There are no tactical manuals for fighter pilots or business leaders to train in compartmentalization. For those of us in the aviation community, we are taught compartmentalization in training, from one pilot or flight lead to the next. It is a tool to enable focus on the mission at hand. Compartmentalization is one of the tactics we share in this book to improve and maximize individual and team resilience. Ours is different from the psychological and medical community's definition. The medical community defines compartmentalization as "a psychological defense mechanism designed to avoid cognitive dissonance." A fighter pilot's version of compartmentalization is simple: if it doesn't have anything to do with this mission—leave it for later. Put it out of your mind to avoid distraction. This means we don't think about our grocery shopping lists, a fight we may have had with a loved one, or a task the boss gave us earlier in the day. Not while flying. Anything that doesn't at once support the flight in front of us is to be put away. 100% of our focus is on mission success.

A good leader knows his people, knows what is happening in their lives. Thus, it is easy to learn of significant life events that cause distraction in the workplace. When we find out about these events, the action should be to clearly communicate team support to this individual. This contributes to his personal resilience, and as a byproduct of the team's collective resilience. This level of support must come from the leader to achieve the greatest effect. Sometimes the situation dictates continued production at work. If time away from work isn't possible or it isn't desired by the individual, then the tactic of compartmentalization applies. It can mitigate any potential risk or harm to the organization or the individual. Some people cannot take time off from work. This can be due to financial obligations, or the situation doesn't call for them not being at work. Supervision and empathy from the team are the combination remedies. This is what allows them to persevere. They will learn, grow, and thrive through adversity. They will improve their resilience. When executed well for one, the team will learn it can apply for all. It is critical to note, whatever the root cause is for the distraction still needs resolution. But it needs attention at the right time by the right professionals. Compartmentalization allows for the continued forward progress of the individual and team. But it is not a long-term solution. Misusing it in that way can come at the expense of, or added damage to, either.

We can't control the tragic events that happen in our lives, but we own the process of handling them. We own that process for ourselves, our families, and as leaders of our organizations. We can mitigate the risks for ourselves and our teammates. We can balance the requirements of the team with the requirements of the individual. Through knowing our people and having empathy for their lives and their families, we can find suitable solutions. The individual, the team, and the mission can continue.

POINTS TO PONDER

8.1. Do you have ongoing events in your life that are distracting and overflowing into other areas of your life like work or home?

8.2. Are you able to compartmentalize those distractions and keep them separate from other parts of your life so you can focus clearly?

8.3. Should those distractions be compartmentalized for short-term benefit, or should they be addressed professionally for long-term health? Who can help you decide?

CHAPTER 9

MOVING FROM VICTIM TO VICTOR

Perspective & Insight of
Luke 'PSYCH' Layman

He left. No warning, he just up and left. At the young age of fourteen I was just short of manhood when my father made the surprising decision to leave my mother. Confusion filled my heart, mind, and body as I recall a single moment in time standing in the kitchen of my North Carolina home. The world was a different place without my father in my daily life. There was very little resilience at all. But really, how could there have been? I had never been taught what it meant to handle adversity. I didn't have enough life experience to draw from to help me understand the pain was temporary. I created mechanisms of resilience through pure determination. If the prestigious "School of Hard Knocks" was the best way to live life, there would be no need for us to write this book or for you to be reading it. I resolved to create success in my own life despite the hand I was dealt.

In the latter years of high school, I learned how to bottle up my frustrations and turn them into high performance. I was an athlete, a scholar student, and on my way to college despite being a child of divorced parents. I was successful by all measures, but not for any level of intentionality. There was no person to model resilient behavior. There was no mentor (much less a parent) to show me what to do with my emotions.

If we take lessons from pop culture, we can look to the not-so-sound advice from the movie *Talladega Nights*. "Bury it deep down in there, and never bring it up again." Most people fail to actively build resilience. They wait until tragedy strikes or a challenge happens, fight through the pain in the moment, then breathe a sigh of relief once it's over—never to look back. This is reactive and results in pain experienced, not lessons learned. The problem with this approach is that the next time tragedy strikes, there is no formula or framework to rely upon. What is needed instead is proactive resilience, using lessons learned to be better prepared for the next challenge, trauma, trip or stumble.

Author Tom Bodett summarizes, "School gives you lessons so you can take the test. Life gives you tests so you can learn the lesson." We all know there are more life challenges ahead. Key to resilience is an acceptance that we will be better tomorrow than we are today because of our learned experiences. As military professionals, we understand it is not the absence of adversity that creates a life worth living. Rather, it's the lessons we learn from our pain that create a meaningful life.

"Difficulties strengthen the mind,
as labor does the body."

LUCIUS ANNAEUS SENECA,
ROMAN PHILOSOPHER

There are two very distinct types of people in this world: victims and victors. The terms are not meant to draw a comparison between tradegies, instead a division of who people chose to react to those tradgedies. History is plagued with abuses and misfortunes to an unwilling party. I know bad things happen to good people. I also know that on the heels of difficult events, we are given one of the greatest blessings in the world—the power of free will. If we have nothing else in our lives, we always have the choice of how we respond.

Those who choose to be victims allow the circumstances of their life to control them. They are reactive, using language like, "Life isn't fair," or "It's different for me. I wasn't born with a silver spoon in my mouth." They continue to wait for bad things to happen and use those events as a scapegoat for why success can't come their way.

On the contrary victors use their circumstances as fuel for growth. They take control of their outcomes by being accountable for their actions, inactions, reactions, decisions, and choices. They know, "I am a better person when I am challenged."

To establish a Warrior Mindset, simply ask yourself, "Will I allow myself to be a victim, or am I determined to be a victor?"

You have already chosen the answer; I am just here to support you. The fact you are reading this book means you have chosen the path of resiliency. I won't argue for your limitations.

Today I am proud to profess I am a victor. But as I entered my senior year of high school, I was still very much a victim. I was angry at pretty much everything. I allowed my anger to be the dominant force in my life, and it served me well. I got pretty much everything I wanted because I belittled the people around me. I entered manipulative patterns that resulted in getting what I wanted. The problem became that the costs were higher than I realized. In my wake of anger, I left broken relationships with my friends and siblings.

Two more decades passed before I realized everything in my life came down to a choice. The choice wasn't whether challenging circumstances and events would occur in my life, but rather how I would respond. Yes, I was the product of divorced parents, a decision in which I had no choice. But the anger was my choice. By the time I learned my lesson for good, I was a husband and father of two. The world demanded a better version of me.

We become victors when we are not only able to deal with adversity, but we welcome it and have gratitude for it. We know that with each challenge we will emerge a better and stronger person. We accelerate growth when there is a path forged in a framework that shortens the length of the pain and transitions quickly to growth.

Although fighter pilots don't have special qualifications or trophies to show for it, most are extremely resilient. In fact, resilience isn't even a word commonly used in a fighter squadron. It's not like we sat around in the vault studying the maximum effective range of surface-to-air missiles and had side conversations about how resilient we were in our free time. Nothing cool about that. Rather, we've built a culture of resilience through a century of fighter aviation experience, though never calling it by name.

Depending on which version of history we read, there are well documented chances of survival on missions that scored in the teens. That means that of the four airplanes that took off, less than one was expected to make it home alive. Luckily for me my chances of survival as a pilot have drastically increased. Technology has become the backbone of survivability. But that's not unique to aviation. Life expectancy in 2020 was 77.3 years, compared to just 29 years in 1820. Advancements in technology, safety enhancements, and modern medicine all contribute to a longer lifespan.

In 1937 there were almost 30 deaths by motor vehicles per 100,000. In 2019, that number was just over 10, despite almost 10 times the number of miles traveled by vehicle. Ten times more miles traveled, three times safer.

Lucky for all of us, the chances of survival have drastically increased. It is a magnificent time to be alive. There is more opportunity than has ever been present in the history of Earth. Information is so readily available that we can learn a new skill or solve a problem with a 10-minute video. Less than three decades ago..." I, too, garnered my knowledge from the family encyclopedia, the public library, and my parents to inform our decision-making. And I am older than I feel Our view of the world could be no broader than that of our parents or the limited information we could gather in print.

Every victor embodies the Warrior Mindset, living with a set of characteristics that allow us to face challenges and move rapidly through them. These following six traits are always present in a victor, and we can sharpen them like a knife each time we are met with adversity.

Self-awareness is comprised of two components: internal and external. Internal self-awareness is the ability to be present to our feelings and emotions. We are constantly applying a litmus test of the events in our world against our own values.

External self-awareness is being present to the world around us. In the study of law there is a term called *proximate cause*. In short, proximate cause is a preemptive occurrence closely related to the actual cause of an event, a concept best understood through illustration. Take for example a car accident. The actual cause of the wreck may be the driver maneuvering the car off the road and hitting a telephone pole. The proximate cause is the deer running across the road that preempted the driver to swerve.

Having high self-awareness means we can fully analyze all the inputs and look for where our actions contributed to the result. If I missed my target while attempting a moving target strafe, it would be very easy for me to scapegoat my 'miss' on poor technology, the target changing directions, or even the atmospherics of the bullet flying through the air. Being fully self-aware allows me to look at both my internal state and the external conditions, accepting full responsibility and being at cause for the miss. Was I stressed or under duress? Did I position my airplane correctly? Did I select the correct tactic or maneuver? By looking at myself first I reclaim the power and acceptance of my role in the outcome.

Confidence. Lack of resilience often starts with a lack of confidence. Amid adversity, we often don't see an immediate way out. If we knew the answer to the problem, we would just act and move past it.

Confidence is derived from past performance. We must stop long enough to reflect on our life and find reasons that we should again be successful. In contrast, a victim may look back on a situation when they were successful and assume that their next challenge will be more difficult and thereby less achievable. As such, they create the conditions for failure and perpetuate their victimhood. Victors have already reasoned that they are following the same process as before, only this time we have more tools in our belts.

Self-Efficacy is a skill you may not have been exposed to before. It is simply our belief as to whether we possess the knowledge, skills, and attitudes necessary to overcome a challenge. This is not bravado, arrogance, or hubris. Conversely, this is very internal. Strengthening our belief that a goal is attainable is only a matter of convincing ourself that the result we want is possible.

The sequence goes like this:

Is it possible?

Is it possible for me?

Is it possible for me, now?

We increase our self-efficacy by looking for reasons to make it possible for us today.

Gratitude is a secret weapon. Have you ever heard someone say, "If I can just get through this, I will change my life?" Displaced gratitude puts thankfulness somewhere in the future. It means that we can only be grateful for what we have today once something changes. This line of thought comes from a victim mentality.

The victor practices gratitude daily. Each day I physically write three things down in my day-planner that I am grateful for. This daily practice creates a habit of looking for things

I love in my life every day, even the days I don't love all the things in my life. When challenges come, I already have a pattern of being grateful for everything in my life, good and bad.

Community can be defined as a group of people with common interests living together within a larger society. There is no stronger sense of community than that found in a fighter squadron. Shared purpose and camaraderie make even the most difficult tasks obtainable.

There is no lonelier place to be in life than singled out in isolation. Resilience can be born simply from a shared experience with others.

Reward. This trait is often the most overlooked. We make decisions in life simply to move toward pleasure or away from pain. The actions that garner the highest reward get our highest attention.

In fighter squadrons, the greatest learning opportunities were in our Roll Call tradition. On Friday night we would gather to tell stories and partake in good food and good booze. It was a ritual more than a party, steeped in history and tradition. It was also our reward for our hard work and an opportunity to celebrate our successes. I could write a whole book about the fighter pilot culture and why tradition is as adequate a reward as any. But Roll Call can most aptly be described by a culture of inclusiveness. We had to earn our way into the club; as such, being a part of the community itself was one of our rewards.

Creating a reward for ourself enables us to intentionally place something in the future to look forward to. It could be as simple as a date night or staycation. By putting something in the future to celebrate our efforts, we create a reason to move forward with optimism.

One final concept rounds out the toolbox of a Warrior Mindset. **Duality,** defined by Oxford Languages as "an instance of opposition or contrast between two concepts or two aspects of something," draws a distinction to a singularly minded approach that forces a person into victim mode. Meaning, when conflict and tragedy strike, a victim tends to view it through a single lens. We often classify events as bad or unfortunate and fail to consider an alternate point of view. Creating duality in our lives allows for something to be negative and have an alternate, positive point of view.

It can be hard *and* it can be worth doing.

We can fail *and* we can learn.

We can yell at our kids *and* we can be a good parent.

We can be sad, dismayed, frustrated, disgruntled, or beat down *and* we can feel gratitude for the place we are in.

We can experience trauma and tragedy *and* have a Warrior Mindset.

POINTS TO PONDER

9.1. Think through one of the biggest challenges you are facing. It could be losing weight, getting a new job or promotion, or finding a deep connection with a loved one. If you fast forward to a time in the future, how will you know you were successful? Take time now to imagine this future version of you, then close your eyes and lean into this future version of yourself.

9.2. Being as specific as you can, identify the reality you envisioned above using all of your senses. At the point of accomplishment, what will you see? What will you hear? What will you smell? What will you touch? What will you taste?

9.3. Once you have this reality in mind, on a scale of 1-10, rate the following:

Is it possible?

Is it possible for me?

Is it possible for me, now?

9.4. Now, focus on the lowest score. To create agency for yourself, you must identify specific steps that make this new reality more attainable. List three actions you can take within the next seven days that will lead you closer to your success.

CHAPTER 10

MORAL COURAGE:
The Essential Personal Attributes of a Resilient Leader

Perspective & Insight of
Robert 'Shark' Garland

"Success is not final; failure is not fatal.
it is the courage to continue that counts."

This pillar of wisdom by Winston Churchill resonates throughout the ages. It speaks directly to our souls, inspiring us to get up, dust off, and move forward...

repeatedly. The determination to move forward exemplifies courage, an internal virtue possessed by many of us.

Effective leaders demonstrate unique courage, illustrated by their ability to act in the face of the unknown, not the absence of it. They make decisions affecting people's lives, their livelihoods, families, and futures. Making conscious decisions to do what is right and good, even when the consequences are difficult displays moral courage, a critical component of resiliency.

The profession of arms, an expressly unique arena, requires exceptional men and women capable of successful leadership to execute in their best capacity. The goal is straightforward: inspire a team to complete tasks and missions in a complex, disruptive, and challenging environment. Conducting missions which are life-altering and possibly life-ending. Simple, right?

The true test of a resilient and morally courageous leader is examined through a series of questions: Will their people willingly follow them? Do followers understand the vision and perform without coercion? Are they loyal? Will they remain by the leader's side in times of risk or danger? People follow when they trust the boss' character and courage above all.

As disclosed in previous editions in the Military Mentorship Mastermind series, the Air Force Weapons School has a motto directing graduates to be humble, approachable, and credible. The purpose of an instructor is to teach, to share knowledge for the sole purpose of enabling the next generation to be better than we are today.

As a new graduate of Weapons School and lead instructor at my squadron, I once forgot the purpose of an instructor. I was blinded to the correct manner by which to teach because of the position I had attained. As one of the top fighter pilots in the United States Air Force I was always right—just ask me at the time! I looked for opportunities to fail a student rather than opportunities to find and promote their successes. I reveled in disciplined teaching instead of appreciating the opportunity to build my students up. My actions fell short of the constructive learning potential.

This changed one day when I overheard a conversation in the squadron hallway. One of the students lamented to another, "Oh no, I have to fly with Shark!" Not excitement, instead disappointment and sorrow. This simple comment struck me to the core. Instead of young eager pilots wanting to fly and learn with me, they hated it. My ego and arrogance had created a persona no one wanted to be around. I failed at my job as an instructor. I failed to effectively pass on the lessons and training others had blessed me with, a gift I was given to share freely with others. With true vulnerability, I admitted I was ineffectual and overbearing. The privilege to teach is a blessing, not an entitlement. We earn credibility through training and experience, but that only affords a foot in the door, an opportunity to share acquired wisdom.

A person can build a thousand credibility bridges but burn only one and fail mightily. Once we gain a certain level of credibility as a leader, then how we behave, treat others, and understand why we are there determines our true impact.

Embarrassment and humiliation are powerful motivators in a life moment. I had to humble myself and admit I was wrong. I took absolute ownership of that fault and publicly apologized to my friends. Admitting shortfalls and mistakes takes moral courage. If we are to achieve Maslow's self-actualization pinnacle of the hierarchy of needs, we must live courageously.

Let's pause a moment and ask, "Why?"

Why should people care about resilient leadership? Because people lead people. Leading, mentoring, and coaching is not merely a science, it is a true art in humanity. William Wood defines the art of leadership in Leaders and Battles as "the means of applying personal ideas affecting the actions of individuals and thus the execution of an organization." He details the goal of a successful leader as one who "encourage[s] others to achieve a greater purpose. A purpose greater than themselves that supports the success of the team."

The art of leadership is also the ability of leaders to express their personalities, thoughts, and beliefs through their work. True leaders mold their leadership style to fit the present situation. In Follow Me II, Major General Newman highlights "military service is a profession, not a craft or a job, but it goes beyond that. Command and leadership are an art, not a skill or technique that can be circumscribed within rules and rigid regulations. Just as a painter must integrate perspective and color to produce his picture, a military commander must balance and merge, push and pull to become a leader."

With this in mind, we must ask ourselves, is the goal of a military leader different than a Fortune 100 CEO? What is the measure of a successful, resilient leader? Is it winning wars or accumulating huge profits? Is it more important to be liked or respected? What defines a successful leader? How does that leader demonstrate moral courage and resiliency?

Another integral aspect of resiliency is moral courage. Resiliency is a mental reservoir of inner strength, a strength which allows us to recover from hardship and deal with the associated stress. Resilient leaders have a continual hunger for knowledge as they fill their quiver of skills with the experience of life, experiences which include proud success of days gone by side by side with the challenges, failures, and losses of yesterday. They learn by being present in each moment, observing and listening to others. These lessons shape a leader's true personality and develop competence and character, which drive our decisions, indecisions, actions, and inactions.

The choices we make reflect our true character and the person we become. Both the military commander and the company CEO face similar choices. One faces success while risking loss of life while the other drives progress with the weight of their team's livelihoods resting heavily on their shoulders. Both leaders are in charge of people. And people live and work with emotion. So, the end result of a challenging decision is the same. Both leaders affect people, their lives and livelihoods, and their future successes or failures.

Resilient leaders have a keen awareness of their situation, their capabilities and weaknesses, as well as those of the people around them. They exercise emotional intelligence and self-control. They see a problem and methodically consider solutions. Emotionally intelligent leaders breathe in through their nose and out through their mouth. They maintain their cool under stress. Calm leaders are confident leaders.

Resilient leaders know failure is a learning opportunity. They are positive and realistic thinkers, intimately familiar with failure. They embrace failure because they know it is a chance to learn and grow. They seek life lessons to make themselves stronger mentally, spiritually, and emotionally. They learn how their whole person reacts in times of trauma. Trauma response fuels the internal mechanism to recover, return, and perform—even when we want to hesitate and give up. It is out of character-building that other personal attributes emerge and are forged through fire. This strength is born in a true belief that tomorrow will be better than today.

Remembering some of the greatest military leaders who motivated individuals to risk their life for our great nation, it becomes evident that these leaders went beyond merely touching the lives of those they inspired. They truly impacted the souls of their followers, motivating each to a calling bigger than one and aligning on the common good. The leaders whom history remembers most, the ones who prevail above all others, are those who won the trust and support of their followers.

A history of warfare informs us of the two most vital qualities of leadership: the ability to make the right decisions and the courage to act on those decisions. It is resolution and determination which enable a leader to stand firm and be resilient when success hangs in the balance. While not visible, moral courage is observed in each leader's demeanor and resolution during times of trial. Moral courage comes from within. An individual's willpower is composed of their personal attributes of confidence and assurance. This same willpower affords a leader the ability to combat the fog and friction of the unknown, allowing them to face the unexpected, especially during times of stress and crisis, and press forward. Press forward with the confidence they made the best decision at that moment with the facts presented to them at that time.

We are all human. We all act and analyze through emotion. In a pivotal moment, I realized the best way to teach and lead is from a humble and approachable position. We can hear or read those words repeatedly, but when we live them, they become very real! If our goal is to promote our people to be the best they can be, to fulfill their calling and true purpose, we must love and care about them. Genuinely. Our people make our mission happen; they enable our success. I consciously remind myself daily from that season forward to think of and serve others first. To see life and work through their eyes. To live humbly.

Leadership is a human endeavor. Leaders must be people who care more for others than themselves. They must risk their own best interests for the betterment of others and the team through selflessness. They care for people and listen more than speak. They strive with all their being to learn from life experiences and develop resiliency. Leaders hold their people's lives in their hands. They must recognize that fact and do all in their power to succeed. And when they do fail or fall short, they must emerge stronger and more capable than before. They must lead from the front with honesty, bravery, and moral courage.

Today, we need examples, leaders, role models, and commanders with the moral courage to stand up and do what is right, to care for their people, and speak the truth. They must hold themselves accountable first; this is owed to those under their charge. Our world needs leaders who have faced adversity, been forged in the fire of challenge, and emerged stronger. Through those trials, through that forging process, a resilient and morally courageous leader can stare any challenge and disruption in the face...and win! In our professional life, I believe there exists no greater calling than the opportunity to lead others. Embrace this blessing with strength and honor.

POINTS TO PONDER

10.1.   We are all human. That means we have the same mental, physical, spiritual, emotional, and social attributes and needs. We are whole when all of these personal needs are in order. Are you whole and complete?

10.2.   The characteristics that make us whole and who we are also empower us to support others. To bless others. To lead others. The Air Force Weapons School shares a tenant of principle: always be humble, approachable, and credible. That ideal is a proven life methodology for success and effective leadership. Are you looking outward, toward another to help them?

10.3.   Historically successful leaders have been emotionally intelligent giants! They are complete inside, affording them the opportunity to focus on other people, not just themself. A powerful leader is at peace in their personal life. Their professional performance is enhanced as a result. They are resiliently forged from life and now possess the moral courage to lead. Your moral compass affords you confidence and empowers you to lead! Spend some time journaling your thoughts with regard to improving your emotional intelligence.

CHAPTER 11

PUTTING THE PIECES TOGETHER: A FLIGHT PLAN TO RESILIENCE

Perspective & Insight of
Robert 'Cujo' Teschner

As we conclude our reflections on how we build resilience, I propose that the mindset we adopt, coupled with the processes we practice and the culture we build, determine whether we're going to be successful in our efforts. I will conclude my reflections by offering several observations from my time in an American Air Force fighter squadron, and then translate these observations into a flight path to resilience for you.

Observation: Flying fighters is a dangerous profession, and things can go really bad, really fast.

As our two F-15s approached the merge, the mission profile demanded we pass one another at an insane rate of speed—I knew we were going to hit. What was interesting was that I was very calm throughout. I experienced fear, but it wasn't fear of death, a death driven by way of a mid-air collision. No, my fear was of something else entirely: sharks. Roughly 115 miles out over the ocean, I knew that after we hit and I safely ejected from my airplane, I would be in the water with sharks. And, thanks to Shark Week, I've come to detest sharks

The mission was one of the basic ones we flew all the time: High-Aspect Basic Fighter Maneuvers—Dogfighting. The idea is to start approximately five miles away from one another, simulate seeing an airplane while unsure whether it's a friend or foe, pass at a very high rate of speed, and then maneuver into a position to kill. It's a high-G loading, extremely physical type of fight, and one I loved.

That day, however, instead of the two of us passing with at least 500 feet of separation, my opponent kept on pointing straight at me. Every time I tried to get some spacing from him, flying my airplane to a position where I had the separation we both needed for a safe and manageable pass…he took it away from me. Five miles burns up quickly when you're flying at 750+ mph, and in a matter of seconds I realized that we were going to hit. Head-on. One hundred fifteen miles out to sea. Damn the sharks.

We both recognized the peril, and we both attempted one last-ditch maneuver, in which time slowed almost to a stop. I had previously heard of people talking about time slowing down in deadly situations, and in that moment I experienced it firsthand. As my adversary's airplane passed mine, I recall making out each individual rivet on the bottom of his fuselage. I noted things I had never before paid attention to on the F-15. It was surreal; it was stunning.

And in a matter of moments, it was over. We missed each another by just a few feet.

Observation: In fighter squadrons we understand and prioritize what's most important. And what's most important to us is constant learning, only always.

At that point in the mission, we were almost completely full of gas. This was the first merge of what was supposed to be three of this type of dogfight engagements. We had at least half an hour of high-G maneuvering ahead of us, and we were there to train for combat. But we had also just lived through a near-death experience; both of us knew exactly what transpired and what it meant. We knew there was no more fighting ahead of us that day…

I called for the "Knock it Off," the radio call that formally ends all tactical maneuvering. As the flight lead, I also called for us to "safe up" our systems, execute a rejoin, and I announced that we were going home. Why? Because after we almost died on a routine training mission that we flew all the time, we both knew we owed it to ourselves to immediately go home to figure out what led to this near disaster. We both knew we owed it to ourselves to debrief this less than 20-second engagement in order to learn. We both understood that doing so was mission critical for our resilience.

Observation: In fighter squadrons we've institutionalized the building of resilience.

The beautiful thing about experiencing life in a fighter squadron is that we have institutionalized a formal approach to resilience, one we practice not just some of the time, but always. Our approach consists of three main components: 1) Mindset, 2) Process, and 3) Culture.

The mindset we've adopted is that of a warrior. We know we're going to win. This remains the case no matter what happens to us out there, no matter how hard it becomes to do so. We do not tolerate victims, and we don't tolerate excuses. We teach and live the Warrior Mindset.

The process we've adopted is one where the mission isn't complete until we've debriefed it. What is a debrief, you might ask? Simply put, it's the place we go to learn from the mission—regardless of whether we won or lost that day—in order to make the next mission better. We have a formal process for debriefing, and we train ourselves through consistent, ritualized debriefs, always.

The culture we've adopted says we need to be vulnerable in the debrief. We need to be open to discussing our failures and our mistakes in order to learn and improve. We must also be humble—free from pride and ego—in order to learn from our failings. And in our culture, we spend time every week talking about what we've learned, sharing by way of a ritual we call Roll Call. There is more to the culture for sure, but these three core tenets help explain how we prepare to be resilient and how we organize to win.

Observation: In fighter squadrons, we expect the worst. We also seek to learn from each experience of pain.

While we truly want things to go brilliantly, we fully expect things to go poorly. Why is this the case? Experience has taught us that almost nothing goes according to plan, and the enemy always gets a vote. A way of translating this last statement into common language is to say life has a way of getting in the way. Because of these factors, we've adopted an approach that helps us learn from each experience. It allows the team to grow, bond, and improve with every new and disruptive experience. I would even go so far as to say that in fighter squadrons we have learned to embrace our failures because we know it's through learning amid failure that we push our limits and become our very best.

On the heels of our near midair collision, my wingman and I knew that we owed it to ourselves and to our tribe NOT to continue to fly but to return home to understand how this near catastrophe took place. We needed to do so in order to prevent ever having that experience again. Our culture demanded that we stop fighting and go home to learn, even if our discussions were only tied to about 20 seconds of flying. That's how seriously we take our work.

Observation: Our culture demands that we practice absolute vulnerability. Not sometimes, but always.

In the midst of our debriefing process, my wingman demonstrated maximum vulnerability from the very get-go. Even before we examined the facts, he immediately shared that he felt responsible for almost hitting one another. He advised he was so focused on winning the fight that he forgot to take the necessary measures to ensure our safety. He was 100% free from pride and ego, along with anything else that would prevent him from learning from his failure. In that moment he demonstrated to me the model of what real leadership looks like. He also enabled the two of us to quickly bounce back from this near disaster, allowing us to return to fly with 100% confidence that the next mission would go better than this one did.

Our story did get better, but not in the sense I wrote about earlier. In this case, on this particular mission, the story got better by the two of us taking the time to sit back, reflect, and analyze how it was that things got so bad so quickly, only so that we would never have to be part of the story of one or both of us dying unnecessarily. Our resilience was enabled by living in a culture that practiced a process through which we learned only always.

I'm alive today because of it.

Observation: A fighter squadron has created an outstanding approach to building resilience. We should follow their lead and do the same in our organizations...

Let's cut to the chase and bring these observations together in a way that advances the cause of building resilience. Here's a proposed flight plan to building resilience:

1. **Implement a Code of Conduct.** Take time as a team and even as a 'team of teams' to define the behaviors you both will and won't tolerate any longer. Give serious consideration to eliminating victimhood. Strongly consider, as well, embracing vulnerability. In all cases, document which behaviors you hold dear, as well as which are no longer acceptable. Then create a Code of Conduct that everyone on each team signs. Define the implications of violating this new Code of Conduct, hopefully with entertaining and interesting approaches that drive buy-in and commitment. Use this process to instill an early version of the Warrior Mindset with your teammates.

2. **Define each team's missions.** Spend time—and this might take a little bit of time—figuring out what your missions are. In my company, we define a mission as an event or process that produces an output, is defined by time, and is an enabler of company success. Once you figure out your missions, craft a team lifecycle around each of those missions. The high-performance team lifecycle consists of tactical-level planning, pre-mission briefings, executing the mission, and then debriefing all of the above. *Ensure no mission is complete until the team*

has debriefed it. And, if you're new to it, understand that a debrief is three things:

a. **The constructive evaluation...**

b. **Of the quality of the team's decisions and associated actions...**

c. **Measured against the objectives the team set out to achieve.**

Again, adopt a ritualized approach to team learning that understands and practices the belief that no mission is complete until the debrief has been conducted.

4. **Learn to embrace failure.** Take time as an organization to define and then collectively highlight failures as a net good. Spend time understanding how failure, properly harnessed, leads to team building, growth, development of trust, and advancing skills. Dr. Amy Edmondson's Harvard Business Review article titled "Strategies for Learning from Failure" would be an outstanding one to dissect as a team and again as an organization in order to fully understand the positives associated with failing well.

5. **Ritualize your own form of Roll Call.** Adopt a ritualized approach to telling stories about winning. Take time to especially celebrate the wins that happened even when the odds were against the team, when it looked like there was no way to win. Take time to publicly recognize those who manifested the Warrior Mindset, even if only slightly, as a way of emphasizing the shift your culture is going to take.

Adopting this flight plan will help you to be proactive in the creation of a learning organization that can bounce back after failure by seeing it for its good and harnessing it to advance your team's cause. Adopting this flight plan will help you to realize the best your teammates have to offer while pushing them to become their best. Adopting this flight plan will help you on your way to *Building Resilience.*

POINTS TO PONDER

11.1.   How well have you prepared your teams to be resilient? If you were to rate your satisfaction on a 10-point scale, what score would you award yourself? Why? What's driving that score? And how does that score compare to your ideal score?

11.2.   Assuming you're not fully satisfied with your score, what is it costing you to not be at your best here? And what is it costing your teammates? Now flip your internal conversation—how would your team benefit from boosting your resilience capabilities?

11.3.   What would keep you from implementing the flight plan outlined in this chapter? If you answer with:

Time: What can you remove from your plate to buy you the time to implement the flight plan?

Team buy-in: How can you work to improve your team's buy-in for adopting a high-performance team approach to resiliency?

Distributed workforce: How can you overcome the challenge of distance and harness technology to adopt the above approach?

Too much is going on: How can you accomplish the current mission sets while finding time to take action on the above?

11.4. How might the approach outlined in this chapter apply to your home team? And how will you take action to build resilience on the home front?

CHAPTER 12

LIFETIME OF LEARNING

Perspective & Insight of
Luke 'PSYCH' Layman

I n January of 1898, a rebellion broke out in Cuba against Spanish colonial rule. The United States became involved in the conflict due to concerns about the treatment of civilians on the island and the potential impact on American business interests. In April of that year, President William McKinley called for volunteers to form a cavalry regiment to support the war effort, and a young man volunteered to lead the group.

The group, formally called the "Rough Riders," was formed in early 1898 shortly after the outbreak of the Spanish-American War. It consisted of a diverse group of men from all walks of life, including cowboys, miners, college athletes, Native Americans, and Ivy Leaguers. The Rough Riders trained in Texas before shipping out to Cuba to join the fight against the Spanish forces.

On July 1, 1898, the Rough Riders and other American troops were ordered to take San Juan Hill, a strategic position held by the Spanish forces. The hill was heavily defended, and the American troops were initially met with heavy resistance. The group's leader refused to stay back with the supply unit and instead led the Rough Riders in a charge up the hill.

Under heavy fire, the Rough Riders charged forward and reached the top of the hill, which gave a decisive strategic advantage to the American forces. This offensive move became one of the most celebrated moments of the Spanish-American War and earned the leader national recognition.

The leader was Teddy Roosevelt, who resigned as Assistant Secretary of the Navy to lead the Rough Riders. He famously said, "The man who is physically and morally clean, alert, and who has a sound body and mind, is the man best fitted to meet any hardship or adversity and to fight his way to victory." This leader, who would later become president of the United States, embodied a "bias for action," coined decades later by General Electric CEO Jack Welch and later made popular by Jeff Bezos of Amazon. The term means you must be decisive, act, and make decisions quickly. Developing a Warrior Mindset requires this same bias in pursuing resiliency. You can read 100 books and not increase your resilience, but you can take a single action and be on the road to a more fulfilled and engaging life.

Our bias for action in fighter aviation follows the same trajectory. The concept "See one, Do one, Teach one" was introduced in the late nineteenth century by William Stewart to train students at Johns Hopkins University's surgical residency program. We use the same approach.

As aviators, we first observe the way others perform. During pilot training, we would observe an instructor pilot demonstrate a maneuver. To learn how to do a loop, an instructor first showed the specific entry parameters, like airspeed and altitude. She said, "We are going to begin with 300 knots of airspeed and 4,000 feet of airspace above us." As I cross-checked the instruments from the tandem cockpit, I began creating the habits that would ensure my success. She pulled the airplane into a nose-high position as the aircraft entered the pure vertical with airspeed decaying until it reached a crescendo of fully inverted flight. At the pinnacle, the airplane was completely upside down. Looking ahead at the horizon, she pulled the airplane through, gaining airspeed and descending back to the starting position. You can gain some understanding of the requirements to complete a loop simply through the words I write. But if it were your turn to execute the maneuver next, you would benefit from seeing me do this in real life.

Building resilience is the same. You model the behaviors of those around you who have attained your desired level of resiliency. If someone is a train wreck, you don't look to them for counsel. To become the most elite version of yourself, you will learn it, you will do it, and then you will teach it. This chapter is the 'learn it,' and your bias for action must include the 'do' and the 'teach.' What I share here is neither intuitive nor natural. You will do this by looking at yourself first, then developing the levels of empathy and awareness to lead others. Even in the infancy of building resilience, you will experience the personal rewards of living a more fulfilled life with a level of intellectual curiosity that opens new levels of happiness, previously unattainable.

here is one hurdle between you and a much better life. Unfortunately, most have never taken the time to understand what is and how it affects every decision you make in your life. It can be defined as your sense of self-esteem and self-importance. The single hurdle is your ego.

This draws a distinction between being egotistical, which carries a clearly negative connotation. Being egotistic is associated with being conceited or excessively absorbed in oneself. But no, the ego is quite the opposite. Every single one of us has an ego. Its job is to sort out what's real and to make sense of the world we see. You've got one—let's put it to work.

Has someone ever blamed you for having too big an ego or told you, "Your ego gets in your way." If so, this chapter will completely reframe everything you *think* you know about your own biases. You will gain a deeper understanding of how others see the world.

To understand the ego, we look to the work of Australian neurologist Sigmund Freud whose 1923 work defines the three parts of our mind. This study of human function identifies the id (pronounced exactly like you think it sounds without an apostrophe), ego and superego. Distinctively these functions are not solely brain-based but comprise the entirety of your operating system at the conscious, preconscious, and subconscious levels.

If being egotistical is considered socially harmful, the ego is neither good nor bad. It is simply your view of the world. It is based on your learned and lived experiences and represents the purest and most authentic version of you. I don't see how that can be bad at all.

According to Freud's Psychoanalytic Theory, the id is the most primitive component and is part of the mind that contains sexual and aggressive drives as well as hidden memories. You are born with this. It is designed to do one thing: keep you safe. It is almost purely subconscious and the driving force of your personality. If the tip of the iceberg you see above the water is your conscious mind, the id is the remainder of the iceberg below the water.

The ego is a matured phase that develops from the id. It validates impulses of the id and creates an acceptable expression in the real world. The filter often helps you keep your mouth closed when you have nothing nice to say. Ego is not your personality. Instead, it is only one component. The ego is like the driver of a sports car. The car has the power and force, but the driver gives it direction and purpose.

The superego operates as a moral compass and begins to form around age five. The first of two parts, the conscience, discerns what society views as good or bad. The second part, ego ideal, includes the rules and standards the ego aspires to.

All three components, the id, ego, and superego, act in conjunction and keep each other in harmony. However, individually they work in isolation and create behaviors that we view as bad. A person with a dominant id would become survival-focused or impulsive. They would act upon their most basic urges with minimal regard for whether their actions were appropriate, much less moral, or legal. An overly dominant superego might lead to a highly judgmental personality.

Let's say you walk into a supermarket while you are hungry and see a delicious hot sandwich. The id suggests immediate consumption of the sandwich to satisfy hunger. At the same time, the superego counteracts that desire by applying a moral direction that says you can't immediately stuff the sandwich in your face.

The key to a healthy ego is a balance between all. Think about your own life right now. Do you tend to be impulsive? Are you historically judgmental? There is no right or wrong; there is simply what is true for you right now and a representation of the best version of you.

In high-performance teamwork, we look at the Plan-Brief-Execute-Debrief (PBED) cycle. This methodology is a key aspect of developing your own Warrior Mindset as it does in any team lifecycle phases or events. There is no secret that mastery for fighter pilots occurs in the debrief. We use a description of the debrief that says, "take the rank off," meaning we intentionally create an environment free of judgment and blame that focuses on the quality of our decisions regardless of the level of any one person's rank.

Building resilience follows the "See one, Do one, Teach one" model. Within the pages of this book, you have discovered characteristics and behaviors of highly resilient leaders with incredible pedigrees and resumes. Individually, each author has described for you a lifetime of learning that compounds during each hardship endured to create a more resilient life. Our approach has no hubris, only a level of curiosity that compels us to believe the best is yet to come.

Resilience is a learned skill. It is best learned by being both a student and a teacher, or better put, a "Player Coach." Being in the game means having a bias for action, being decisive, and making quick decisions. When adversity strikes, which it will, what is your action plan? Are you building habits with each level of stress or confrontation that will lead you to a 1% better life?

There are three steps to creating a habit of resiliency.

1. **State the problem.** You can't fight what you can't see. You find yourself overwhelmed when things start to go wrong. It feels like everything is piling up or the odds are stacking up against you. Perhaps a few things need attention, but it's not a matter of swinging away on everything at once. Instead, it's a matter of figuring out what alligator is nearest to the boat and acting decisively. When stating the problem, be specific. What about the problem is challenging? What impact is this adversity having on your life? What are the contributing factors that are making the situation worse?

2. **Accept your role.** Are you a victim or a victor? In any adverse situation, you must stop and look at the part you play. By accepting responsibility, you put power back into your ability to overcome any challenge. Adversity comes in all shapes and sizes, but how we respond is where our true freedom begins.

3. **Identify the outcome.** What would you like to happen? If you get mired down in the circumstances, you will continue to focus on the challenges. You don't get what you want in life; you get what you tolerate. By setting your intentions on a future state you desire, you begin to move your focus toward that outcome. Where your intention goes, your attention follows; where your attention goes, your energy flows.

By discovering our own biases, we can show empathy toward others in the exploration of their own. The same questions we ask ourselves become the foundations for success in leading others.

The entry point in any discussion on resilience is very simple: grace. We owe ourselves the grace that we are doing our best and working to make 1% changes in our lives. Extending that same level of grace to those around us creates bonds for a more resilient team. When we ask the same questions of them that we ask of ourselves, we transition from player to coach. Because you are now armed with the mechanics of resiliency, you can lead others. You now have the upper hand because you have knowledge reserved for high-performance teams. As you lead conversations with others going through challenging situations, you must do so with a level of understanding and empathy that allows them the same sense of discovery you have achieved.

You can rest easy knowing you are doing the work on yourself and leaving behind a trail of better humans.

POINTS TO PONDER

Now is the time to do the work.

12.1.   State the problem.

Humans speak in distortions, deletions, and generalities. We do it to facilitate communication ease and help others understand our case. But often we critical points of our story that would help others better understand us. Make sure your statement details the pertinent facts. Be critical of yourself and don't withhold information-especially if it may appear vulnerable.

12.2.   Ask yourself if the problem statement as written is completely true? What would make it more true? If I were to act as an impartial observer of your statement, what questions would I ask to gain more clarity and more granularity?

12.3.   Accept your role. When you look at the problem statement above, how do you react when you believe that statement?

12.3.   Take the time now to figure out your level of responsibility in the situation. No matter how insignificant, it's important for you to have accountability for the role you are playing in the event.

12.6.   Think through what an acceptable outcome would be, even if it isn't your perfect outcome. You'll be surprised how much ground can be gained if you can clearly articulate what you want to happen. Spend some time journaling your acceptable outcome.

CHAPTER 13

PURPOSE: THE PILLAR OF A RESILIENT LIFE

Perspective & Insight of
Robert 'Shark' Garland

Why am I here? Why is my life important? From our youth to today and extending into tomorrow, each of us asks these internal questions countless times. Am I supposed to be something in life? The answer is: YES! You are special, created for a specific purpose for as long as you draw each breath. Your life experiences have led you to this moment, and not by accident. Purpose is your North Star, a point of focus which guides and encourages, enabling confidence that what you are doing is right and meaningful. It is your foundation. Purpose leads to resilience.

There is a state of being that encompasses the unique features of what makes us who we are. It is the human condition known as the *whole person*. We are each subject to it. It points us toward the meaning of life and our sense of curiosity about the world around us.

The principles of the whole person concept are simple. Create a life grounded spiritually, mentally, physically, and emotionally. It is about becoming the best person you can be—enjoying your life along the way, and as a result, becoming your very best in the areas in which you are naturally gifted and talented. This is *your calling*.

These foundational principles, when applied to your personal life and professional work, will benefit your family, your business, your community, and all of us collectively. They have the power to transform and inspire your human condition. These principles center on attributes such as integrity, service to others, personal responsibility, and humility. They fuel the relentless pursuit of excellence. It is bedrock on which to build your personal resiliency.

HOW DO YOU FIND YOUR PURPOSE?

First, believe you exist for a reason. That underlying faith builds confidence in the knowledge of who you are and that what you do has meaning. Second, what are your talents? You were born with natural God-given skills and abilities—your aptitudes. These gifts are unique to you. They afford you the ability to perform tasks and create solutions others cannot. Few can throw a fastball like Nolan Ryan or dunk like Michael Jordan. Not many can sing like Carrie Underwood. Your aptitudes point toward your purpose. The famed psychologist Abraham Maslow calls these self-actualized people, *peakers*. They are courageous, creative, willing to take risks and make mistakes, and display sincere humility.

Knowing your purpose is a doctorial level of emotional intelligence. It sets the stage for personal resiliency and success. It empowers you to make the correct decisions and associated actions that align with the goals of the team. When other team members do the same, the result is extremely high performance on tasks. Everyone understands their purpose and the purpose of the team. We can see the good in our work and the difference it makes to others. When we define and apply a clear and just team purpose, members can apply their own gifts, skills, and passions to the work. We are inspired to serve by giving our best every day. The team wins!

Good leaders care for their people first. People do not need a list of things they should and should not do. They need a living, breathing example. The best sermons in life are lived, not preached. Watching how someone else lives daily has far more impact on us than receiving an emailed list of rigid rules and laws.

Today, we need positive role models, coaches, mentors, and servant leaders more than ever, those whose selfless actions and understanding of what is right and just sets an example for others to emulate. Your life may be the only book some people read. With that realization comes heavy responsibility. Aristotle once said, "Excellence is an art won by training and habituation. We do not act rightly because we have virtue or excellence, but we have those because we have acted rightly."

The constant pursuit of excellence is a unique attribute of personally and professionally successful people. It is something that traditionally makes us as Americans unique—the pursuit of impossible dreams and our constant drive to improve. It is a ceaseless, relentless pursuit of excellence that makes us exceptional.

When I learned of my selection to be the Air Force Weapons School Commandant, the excitement was overwhelming…a dream come true! In short order, I was punched in the face with the realization of the task, the responsibility to be the lead instructor for the whole Air Force and to help Air Force corporate leadership transform and inspire our nation's combat power. My task was to train the next generation of experts. Simple…

I spent the six months leading up to assuming the job studying and thinking about how to inspire our instructors and students to fulfill their purpose to be the absolute expert in their specialty, the next generation of exceptional instructors. I remembered lessons my grandfather and father taught me. I remembered my mother's words of wisdom. And, I looked back through my career at notes and experiences I had collected. Then it hit me! If I knew at the beginning of this journey what I know now, would my resilient life be even stronger? So, I wrote a note... a letter for myself at the beginning.

I am writing you this letter to share thoughts of wisdom to help prepare you for this journey. As you read this, I trust you recognize some truths, some guiding principles, and some timeless advice, some encouragement, experiences, and even some correction.

Your word and your handshake define your integrity, your name, your values, and your beliefs. Watch your words, because you cannot withdraw them. Your intuition, when the hair on the back of your neck stands up and you hear that quiet voice—always listen!

You will learn you are judged by your actions and behaviors. Strive to be healthy spiritually, mentally, physically, and emotionally. Count yourself blessed when you are privileged to speak and share a story.

You will use words like integrity, honor, and faithfulness. These words will represent who you are. A life spent defending something important to you. Remember, others have served before you and they paved the path you see ahead. Their example of moral courage is available for you to exemplify. It will take your devotion to demonstrate that same moral courage on your journey so hold the line and stand tall!

Listen more than you talk. Read and study so when you face a decision, you are prepared. When your wingman yells "break right!" move without hesitation because if you don't, you will die.

Understand who your friends and loved ones are and speak their language, not your own. Please know that while your words have weight, people always remember how you make them feel. Compassion and attention are your keys to success.

When you are given the awesome responsibility to lead people, care for them first! Your company has a mission, but remember it is your people who do the work. Inspire and empower them and watch success SOAR! When they succeed, you succeed. Embrace failure. Fail often and know it is a terrific opportunity to gain experience. To improve and to be better tomorrow. Demonstrate humility as you learn. Hold yourself and your team members accountable. Treat others with dignity and respect. I promise you will need their hand one day.

As you sit here today, your future is limitless. Dreams, goals, and aspirations are countless. The question is: do you want to be successful in life; a successful leader, commander, or business owner? While you focus on a specific task, please believe success is much bigger than the single accomplishment. Success requires an indelible commitment to two rules: care for others and always do your best! You are going to fail; embrace it and learn. Each lesson learned will build on your foundation of purpose. You will understand how to be resilient. These will be the moments on your journey you will remember. Recognize them as they occur and take the time to be there.

Your future is bright! While you may wonder what your purpose is today, know this...life is a journey, not a destination. When you get your first job, that is just the beginning. Do your best in that moment. You will never be there again. You will make friends that last a lifetime. You will gain experience that you will tell stories about when you are old. Cherish every moment even amid arduous work.

When you look back on this journey, I trust you will smile. You have a challenging journey ahead. You are following greatness, and many are counting on you to win. Pave the path of greatness for those behind to follow. Then, when your time nears an end, and you call "Full Stop" for the final time, you will know you gave your best.

This letter is about you, your values, your beliefs, your ideals. It is about your future. Your service and commitment to excellence. I trust this helps you realize your purpose early. Armed with this knowledge, you will be best prepared for what lies ahead. Opportunity and challenge, joy and disappointment. You are armed with the ability to overcome. Because, in truth, when you look back on the best parts of your journey, you will realize it was never about you at all. That is the core pillar which builds a resilient life.

POINTS TO PONDER

13.1.   If you were to write a letter to yourself, offering advice on life and success, what would it say?

13.2.   Why are you here? Why is it important? These are the basic fundamental questions of life. Do you have a purpose? How do you know?

13.3.   Knowing, understanding, and believing you have a purpose and what it is defines your life baseline. This is your 'why.' It is unique to you. Clue in on your purpose. Consider your personal gifts, natural talents, and acquired skills. Activities you thoroughly enjoy doing. Activities that energize you! When you are doing what you were created for, you soar in both your personal and professional life!

13.4.   We all face challenges in life. We grow and mature our resilient character with each experience: good or bad. With the confidence of owning your purpose in life, you are empowered to quickly recover and soar to even greater heights tomorrow. Tomorrow will always be better than today. And with your power to overcome, you are free to carry your brother! Your purpose driven life is a resilient life. Spend some time journaling the details of your purpose driven life.

CHAPTER 14

THE IMPORTANCE OF FAMILY RESILIENCE

Perspective & Insight of
Brian 'Stickit' Emme

A Warrior Mindset is not reserved solely for the individual deploying. It is not the sole purview of those who walk out the front door to board a ship or pilot a plane for months at a time away from home and family. The spouse who stays has equal rights to the title of Warrior, and equal qualifications to the associated mindset that comes with handling the home business in the wake of separation. It's a team effort. Some teams flourish, while others flounder. So, what differentiates the two? What are the key elements that enable one family to successfully navigate this life challenge and others fall short? Time has taught us the secret to our family's success. But we didn't always have this recipe. Trust, intentional communication, and a support network are three critical tenets of family resiliency.

After a 25-year military career, the box score will show: 11 deployments overseas and a total of 53% of my career spent away from home. Our nuclear family consists of my wife, a working mom and Navy spouse, and our two children. Each child was born on islands outside the contiguous United States. Our son Jake was born in Japan and our daughter Isabel was born in Hawaii. The away time includes more than the deployments, which often lasted 6-10 months at sea. It includes months of temporary assignments to training locations in preparation for those deployments. Professional schooling, conferences, and travel days round out more days spent away.

We signed up for this. To be clear, I signed us up for this. My wife Lisa joined the adventure five years after I first became a Naval officer. My attempts to explain the totality of the separation were likely lost in translation. In the early years, she would often flinch each time I told her it was time to go. That flinch transitioned over time to a solemn nod. Her commitment to me and the United States Navy, like so many spouses before her, and in all our sister services, is unquestionable and honorable. She served her country alongside me.

TRUST

Trust either builds or erodes over time, accelerated by separation in both directions. Young couples often struggle with the time and distance that separates them. Many strong couples find their breaking points during those separations. Hundreds of reasons pave the road of separation for well-intentioned couples. For our family, our strength lay in the trust we had in each other. Trust in the belief that each was doing the best they could under those arduous circumstances on behalf of the other. Trust built after every successful deployment.

For my part, I had to believe, and I did, that she was holding down the fort to the best of her ability. Since I wasn't there to help, I didn't get to judge her decisions or actions. Rather, the offer of support and thanks from afar was the only successful possibility. Easier said than done. I came home far too many times and asked 'why' this or that had happened or 'why' this or that was the response. Those homecomings typically ended poorly for me. I learned to start smiling more as I walked back in the door. I held any comments I may have had if I disagreed with the outcome. A few walls were painted in colors I would not have chosen over the years! It was more important for me to understand and empathize. I was the outsider from 15,000 miles (about 24140.16 km) and six months away from the realities of life at home for a family of four minus one. Trust was the coin of the realm for our family during deployment. Even if we had access to phones and email, the fact that I wasn't physically there was reason enough to defer decisions and judgement to my teammate who was there each day getting the job done at home. This mindset empowered and strengthened our relationship.

INTENTIONAL COMMUNICATION

Intentional communication differs from talking to the degree that thought goes into the expected outcome of the conversation. It plays a pivotal role in balancing the stress of separation. Nothing will lift spirits like seeing a note from home. "Mail is morale" is an understood phrase for deployed service members. But the contents of the message are equally as important to manage. Intentional communication can either strengthen or deteriorate the bonds of a relationship.

Often in the early years, we would try to replicate our long-distance discussions as if we were sitting across the dinner table. But what was lacking in our attempts to replicate those discussions was time and perspective. We didn't have the time to fully discuss each nuance, and without being there in person, I often failed to fully understand the details. This would lead to disagreements over courses to choose. And without the benefit of being there to see it and understand all the intricacies of the situation, it was impossible to fully help in choosing the solution. My frustration would build because of not feeling helpful. She understood over time to discuss only those topics that needed discussion or decision. If it was an issue she could handle without bringing it up, she handled it. That helped me avoid the stress of worrying over items I had no control over while gone. That mindset enabled me to focus on the tasks at hand, which maximized the odds of successful completion. Countless comrades struggled to solve problems placed on them from spouses afar. The stress and weight literally wore on their faces daily. This tactic also served to build her confidence and capability to handle things without requiring my input. We could focus our intentional communications on us and less on the stuff and events around us.

A SUPPORT NETWORK

My wife is independent and self-sufficient. She can accomplish tremendous feats at home and at work, often simultaneously. Most people can be very capable for short periods of time. Few can be successful for the better part of a year at that elevated level without a little support. There were small techniques I could employ to ease stress and help in the processes of home life, like paying bills or getting oil changes completed ahead of time. Others included pre-arranging for lawn or house care. Leaving hidden presents can create an instantaneous scavenger hunt that lift spirits when times get tough. But the most effective tool is having a support network.

Leveraging friends, neighbors and family has been most critical to our success. When our children were young and each was mobile and fast, having two parents around to be in a one-on-one defense was key. One parent trying to zone up against our two little ones proved unsuccessful. They were too fast and covered far too much ground to keep them safe—we had to call in support! That support often came in the form of grandparents, neighbors, or hired help. We cannot over-thank our grandparents for the days, weeks, and collective months they supported our family over the years. They would drive or fly in from many miles away when we asked for their help. We recognize we were extremely fortunate to have their willing help, as not all families have that support structure readily available. We also called in many favors with friends and neighbors locally when errands, sports practices, or making meals became overwhelming. Often, the spouse network from the unit deployed was used on a rotational basis as each understood the unique challenges the others were navigating. Lastly, we had to rely upon hired help in the form of caregivers when Lisa had to travel for her own work. We often had to go this route after having exhausted our friend and family network. Hired caregivers was not a tool used as relief from the home requirements, but as help with those requirements. Often times after a long deployment upon my return, she would sleep as if she hadn't in months! Once the collective strain was removed, and the passing of the baton completed, it was time for a long, and well-deserved, nap!

Military families form strong networks of support while navigating the same challenges together. Families who use support networks always fare better than those who don't. Leveraging that support, regardless of where it comes from is always helpful, but it's not always available. Resilience and strength are developed through repetition and the courage to ask for help.

Trust, intentional communication, and using a support network enable military families to navigate separation with success. It enables them to thrive through deployments and separations. Thinking and planning ahead can only last as long as the list of creative ideas. It's creating the Warrior Mindset at home, supported by the warrior abroad, that enables family resilience. Children will learn this pattern through experiencing it firsthand from their parents. Thus, the cycle of learning resilience continues.

POINTS TO PONDER

14.1.   If you had to leave home and everything you are responsible for there for three days, three weeks, or three months, could you? Who or what would you have to leave in place to cover in your absence?

14.2.   Have you built a support network to help you navigate a deployment? Have you done so with enough time that this network would be willing to step in and help?

14.3.   Are you willing to put your trust in your team to handle issues in your absence and accept the outcome of their decisions in your stead?

14.4.   How do you prepare for a conversation to ensure you are intentional about what is said? Will you have notes, and will you patiently stick to them as the discussion shifts? What is the intended outcome of those discussions?

CHAPTER 15

WHAT NOW, WHAT NEXT

Perspective & Insight of
Chris 'Elroy' Stricklin

A s a fighter pilot, the art of the debrief is a required skill set we hone each and every day. each and every flight. It complements the other aspects of the Plan-Brief-Execute-Debrief (PBED) cycle that governs our every action, inaction, and reaction. Every mission begins with a plan, one which details the clearly defined and universally understood mission objectives along with our detailed path to success. It defines the end goal, details the starting line, then designs the journey between the two. With the finish line constantly in mind, we map the steps from today to the goal to connect the two non-negotiables. Next, we brief the group that will execute the mission as a high-performing team. Everyone must understand who does what by when on this journey. The third phase is the adrenaline-filled execution of high-speed, high-G maneuvers coordinated between skilled pilots like a perfect ballet of talent. Finally, we wipe the sweat from our brow and reconvene for the most important aspect of a high-performance team, the debrief. Again, opening with purpose, the debrief is a nameless and rankless review and assessment of what went right and what went wrong, along with a precise understanding of 'why' for each with a root cause analysis.

The purpose of a debrief is to enable us to duplicate our successes and learn from our shortfalls, to develop lessons learned that will improve future execution and performance. It is that simple, and it is also that complex. While this introduction details a high speed explanation of the PBED Cycle, there is so much more to each aspect which will be covered in other volumes of this series. Experts have devoted their entire careers and entire lives to advancing these concepts. While all of the authors of this book are proven craftsmen of these concepts, one stands above the others.

Robert "Cujo" Teschner was the advisor on what became the military standard for fighter operations in the 10 June 2006 United States Air Force Weapons School Dissertation, "Methodology of the Debrief." This 23-page work details the art of the debrief, which includes Mission Reconstruction, Debrief Focus Points, Contributing Factors, Instructional Fixes, and so on.

My favorite quote across the pages establishes a "systematic approach... to use when running... debriefs to ensure the quality of each debrief is the best it can be. The intent... is to show the same debrief methodology applies regardless of mission type. It is also the intent... to show this methodology will help ensure the same quality of debrief regardless of what type of mission was flown." While this is my favorite, it is also the point of growth from which this methodology had capacity to grow into life-impacting operations.

While young Cujo knew the universal application of these principles to every mission we flew, the experiences of his youth landed him short of the true applicability of the methodology to another mission set: *life*. As combat-proven military leaders, our authors and other military members now utilize this same methodology to grow in *every* aspect of our lives. To be better tomorrow than we are today.

First, plan. Plan for the success you define. Plan for what can go right and what will go wrong, along with your initial actions when each does. Stand in front of a whiteboard. On the right side, define success in your life—what it is, what it includes, how to know when you get there, and when you must achieve it. This is your mission objective for life. Next, define today on the left side—where are you and what you have or don't have for skills. Analyze these two points in detail. Ask yourself: What will cause you to fail? What could derail your path to success? Understand your strengths, the tools in your arsenal, and the team that supports you. These are your resources, which will enable your success. Also, detail the resources you will need to acquire, skills or connections, which will accelerate your chances of success. Incorporate lessons learned thus far in your life, from books you read or those you respect to mentor you in this life journey.

The difficulty begins as you map the journey between the two, knowing it will not be a straight line, instead one with detours, mountains, valleys, off-ramps and on-ramps. This will become your course of action for life, which will map success, every effort and action, step by step and task by task, from today to the finish line. At this point, many ask for more on the military course of action explanation. Looking to military guidance and procedure we find:

A military course of action (COA) is a set of possible plans or strategies that military commanders and their staff consider and analyze in order to achieve a specific military objective. A COA is developed through a deliberate planning process that involves the identification of the mission, the evaluation of the situation, the development of different options, the analysis of risks and potential outcomes, and the selection of the best option or combination of options to achieve the mission.

A COA is usually presented in the form of an operational plan, which includes the specific tasks, timelines, resources, and responsibilities required to execute the chosen course of action. It is designed to be flexible, adaptive, and responsive to changes in the situation or the enemy's actions. A military COA is an essential tool for military planning and decision-making, as it enables commanders to anticipate and prepare for different contingencies and challenges that they may face in the field.

As you ponder the journey, label the checkpoints of life; understand each chapter of the book of life you are authoring. Assign the tasks which must be accomplished to enable this journey of success. Understand the progress needed at the end of each season of life, closing one chapter as you begin the next. Finally, review your threats to success. Look back to the list of what could go wrong and the forces which are working against you. Analyze the impact and ramifications of each, understanding how each will affect your journey. Then detail your immediate actions if one should occur. Clearly establish the first three immediate actions needed in an emergency. These will form your reaction while buying you decision space to determine follow on actions.

This cycle of action, this construct of success, forms the basis of how we live our lives. It enables us to examine our lives to improve our lives. This has always been a joke in the Stricklin house with our four military kiddos. Disney World has always been the most magical place on earth for me, and I am determined to be successful when we vacation there. Before we travel, we plan our attack to include start time, breaks, and the path of our progress through the park detailing the order in which we will experience each ride and the time best-suited for line management. As a family, we brief the plan as we ride out of the Disney Transportation Center. As the characters drop the rope to allow entry to the park, our execution begins. The funny part of the story occurs as we board the monorail for the day's end trip back to our hotel. With weary, exhausted faces one of the children looks at me and asks, "Okay Dad, how can we vacation harder tomorrow?" At this point the family debrief begins.

While this is a jovial and true family story, it does not detail the heavier aspects of our life which must be debriefed. This work is about resilience, how we embrace challenges and emerge stronger on the other side. This is where the military methodology reigns supreme. As I was recently talking someone through the Life PBED Cycle mentioned above, he called me one morning and alleged I singlehandedly kicked off his mid-life crisis with the methodology. He went on to detail a trauma experienced many years back, one which concluded with a loss of life. Speaking through tears in his heart, he detailed how this situation, which he had considered fully dealt with back in the day, was weighing heavy each time his thoughts remembered. My advice, with foundations in my own trauma from years gone by, was that any event weighing heavy on your heart should be addressed. In addition, many people think they have dealt with trauma, past tense. In reality, dealing with trauma will remain an action. Dealing with trauma and growing through it always has three aspects, including the past, present, and future. How you have dealt with a situation in days gone by? How are you dealing with it today? And how do you pledge to deal with it in the future? The clarity of mapping out your tomorrows on the journey of life always forces an examination of days gone by. Do you have lessons learned as you grow or only lessons experienced?

In addition to the Life PBED shared above, we must uniquely address each and every trauma, every accomplishment, and every struggle in life. Here's how:

Step One: Honesty & Openness.

Openness to address every aspect of an event and honesty with your analysis of each event, honesty with yourself on the facts of the event, along with your accountability in its occurrence. Accept and acknowledge your feelings and embrace the emotion.

Step Two: Confidence & Commitment.

Examine how you have examined the experience in the past. View the event through a lens of positivity. Reframe the moments as an opportunity for growth and learning. In Cujo's words, look at the moments and remind yourself, "my story just got better." Do this with confidence that you are strong enough to handle the event in a manner which confidently permits growth. We are not what happens to us in life; we are who we become after it happens. Our today is the culmination of our yesterday and the lessons learned from each experience; both the good times and the trying ones define who we are. We determine who we become from each of these moments. Be confident as you paint your tomorrow on the blank canvas of life revealed with each new sunrise.

Step Three: Embrace the 4 Whys.

As a trauma survivor, I find people tend to ask themselves three questions after a traumatic event:

Why did this happen?

Why did this happen now?

Why did this happen to me?

For those who have not faced impending death or life altering traumatic events, these questions still apply to smaller stumbles or missteps in life. While these questions are important to acknowledge and understand on your journey to learn from each, the most important question remains to be addressed:

Why did I survive?

This fourth question is the one which empowers growth, learning, and improvement. This is where lessons learned are addressed and incorporated in our tomorrow. This is a deep question which forces an analysis of our path in life, of how we become stronger from the event and how we can best grow through it, for it, and from it.

Step Four: Empower your team.

No fighter pilot stands alone. We stand on the shoulders of giants, those who came before us and passed their knowledge to us to enable higher levels of success. We rely on mentors who encourage our growth and development and empower us to be more tomorrow than we were today. The question is, "If this is how I become the best fighter pilot in the world, why would I not utilize these same principles in life?" Find your group of mentors, people who you trust fully with your deepest feelings and ones who are connected to you through shared experiences. As we assembled the influencers whose names appear on the cover of this work, we did not fully understand our connection in the beginning. We did not understand how connected we would truly become on the journey of authoring this work. Our conversations routinely turned to being purposeful peers for one another, not in writing or researching. We grew from and embraced our shared traumatic experiences.

Step Five: Positive reflection.

As you look back to the events of days gone by, allow your mind to focus on the growth each enabled. Detail how your life is better by having each experience, but don't dwell on the negatives. As time goes by, these positive reflections will cement the memories of the positive effects while mitigating the negative ones.

Step Six: Cultivate a growth mindset.

Our resilience means growing through our experiences, not merely enduring the pain but blossoming from it. This process propels us beyond our ability to tolerate a trauma and involves our capability and capacity to emerge a stronger person, or a higher performing team, on the other side of the challenge.

For us, each challenge in life is a chance to learn, to grow and to improve. For us, our story gets better through each success, trauma, and steppingstone on this journey and adventure of life. From each experience, embrace gratitude, empower growth, and enable giving. Embrace the gratitude for your survival, an appreciation for the opportunity to see the tomorrows you almost lost. Empower growth through the clarity you receive from the events, the confidence you can be better tomorrow than you are today, and the commitment to improve at each sunset as you reflect on the experiences gone by. Enable giving to share your gifts with those around you. Whether it be openness on dealing with trauma, details of how you deal with your trauma, or a comforting shoulder for others dealing with trauma, pay it forward.

Resilience is a skill requiring continuous improvement and dedicated intentionality. The art of resilience does not mean there is no pain along the journey. It means there is gain that follows the pain, or accompanies the pain, as we each continue to deal with the shadows following us in a life containing all our moments, days, and experiences.

POINTS TO PONDER

15.1.   How do you define success in life? A true definition is not as shallow as a pay raise or promotion; it is one which encompasses your life in its entirety. A true definition of success in life is one that you will judge your life against, every action, inaction, and reaction, as you inhale your last breath on this earth.

15.2.   What is your 'why' in life? Different than a simple definition of success, this reminds you why you are here, why you devote your time to the people and efforts you do. Your 'why' in life should be no more than five words in length and should apply to every aspect. With each decision, project, or time commitment, ask yourself: "How does this align with my why?" If it does, then continue. If it does not, ask yourself why you are doing it.

15.3.   What are the most important tasks in your current season of life? There should be only five and they must be put in order of priority. This will allow you to properly allocate your most important resource of time.

15.4.   What are the tasks critical to accomplish during this season of life? They could be large items like retirement, or small ones like taking your wife to see the penguins of Patagonia. Develop a to-do list for life and work toward those goals. You will also feel intrinsic accomplishment once checking them off.

CHAPTER 16

MOVING FORWARD ON BUILDING RESILIENCE

And so, it ends. This chapter marks the official completion of our short and hopefully compelling reading journey, one that included the exploration of mindset and process, creating a flight path to *Building Resilience*. Congratulations: We completed this journey in the equivalent of a short flight. We were able to cover *a lot* of important ground on this short flight, doing so by way of stories some of us have never before shared in written form. We sincerely hope you enjoyed the trip.

Allow us now to briefly address an element none of us tackled deeply in writing this book. Specifically, we didn't directly address the impact faith has in *Building Resilience*. We didn't address how using faith is a necessary component for being ready to bounce back. For many of us, faith is *the* most vital element in the development of that which builds resilience. It also happens to be a really big topic and one deserving of its own focus. We felt we could afford to leave it out of this book with an eye toward addressing it in the future. Anticipate that some of us will do exactly that, and we'll do our best to keep you posted on how that piece develops.

Returning then to the fact that we've ended this part of the journey, you might be inclined to ask, "What now?" Benjamin Franklin once said, "Well done is better than well said." For us authors, our satisfaction is not achieved in you reading what we wrote. Our sense of joy—our belief that we've made a difference in writing this book—is rather found in **you doing** what we've shared as part of your own approach to *Building Resilience*. Pulling from another founding father Thomas Jefferson, "Nothing can stop the man with the right attitude from achieving his goal; nothing on earth can help the man with the wrong mental attitude." Mindset matters. What's yours? Having now completed the pages of this book, what's your mental attitude when it comes to intentionally *Building Resilience*? We truly hope your attitude is best summarized as this, "I now have a bias for action! I can't wait to get started!"

Let's return to the guidance of Benjamin Franklin as he famously remarked, "Tell me, and I forget. Teach me, and I remember. Involve me, and I learn." What is interesting and amazing for our five authors is how we developed a true sense of community as we began this journey together. We believe the same holds true for you to some extent. As readers, you might have found that you had a small sense of community with the authors, one that lasted for as long as it took you to read our chapters. You identified with us, with some more than with others, and then a sense of bonding may appear to hit an abrupt end commensurate with the last page of text.

This is an important element that deserves our attention. Please know this: We firmly believe it's through community we make progress in adopting the approaches outlined in these pages. It's in building a community in which we involve one another and begin to learn. And so, we would like to welcome you to our newly founded and soon-to-be-growing community of resilience practitioners. The best way to join us is through this QR code:

The idea of accessing our community is driven by the belief that *it is through organizing in teams that we maximize our resilience*. For it is through the process of *actively teaming* that we lift each other up, help one another when we fall, and support one another through the struggles and challenges we face in life. We believe so deeply in the concept of helping people build resilience that we're building the corresponding community to assist in this practice.

And so, our online site is where we'll go to continue to explore, learn, and grow. It's where we'll share—by way of both video and text—how it is that we're taking action on building resilience in our organizations. The ambition here is robust, and it's going to take work to do what we can envision. But we'll start small and build from there, doing what we can only because our teammates need us to do so. Our teammates need us to help them build resilience. And all of us benefit by finding ways to build hope for a better tomorrow. All we ask is that you join us.

Finally, and in return to our Foreword, please remember that **each author wrote this book for *you*. *You*** were always on our collective minds as we wrote our chapters. It's **your ability to lead** confidently, with enthusiasm and vigor, even amid nonstop pain points and disruptions, that focused our writing and caused us to share with incredible vulnerability what we've chosen to share. Our world *desperately needs good leaders,* solid leaders, steady leaders, accountable leaders, and inspirational leaders—our world needs *real leadership* **now more than ever before in our lifetimes**. We want to help *you* to be who the world needs you to be, and a huge part of your leadership ability is dependent on you building your resilience.

So welcome to the world of resilience builders! Welcome to your online team! Together, let's start *Building Resilience* in a world that desperately needs it!

"We are what we repeatedly do.
Excellence, then, is not an act but a habit."

THE STORY OF PHILOSOPHY

#LeadIntentionally

&

#LiveIntentionally

BIBLIOGRAPHY

"Benjamin Franklin Quotes." BrainyQuote.com. BrainyMedia Inc, 2023. 26 April 2023https://www.brainyquote.com/quotes/benjamin_franklin_383997

"Plan, Brief, Execute, Debrief." All Hands, 18 Jun. 2019, allhands.navy.mil/Stories/Display-Story/Article/1879711/plan-brief-execute-debrief/.

"Thomas Jefferson Quotes." BrainyQuote.com. BrainyMedia Inc, 2023. 26 April 2023. https://www.brainyquote.com/quotes/thomas_jefferson_120994

"Tom Bodett Quotes." BrainyQuote.com. BrainyMedia Inc, 2023. 26 April 2023. https://www.brainyquote.com/quotes/tom_bodett_394336

1973, They Call Me Coach by John Wooden, as told to Jack Tobin, (Epigraph of Chapter 17), Quote Page 112, Bantam Books, New York. (Front matter states that an edition from Word Books was published December 1972) (Verified with scans)

Churchill, Winston. Commencement Speech, 26 Feb. 1946, University of Miami, Florida. Speech.

Clifton, Jon. Blind Spot. Gallup Press, 2019.

Edmondson, Amy Dr. "Strategies for Learning from Failure." Harvard Business Review, Apr. 2011.

Freud, Sigmund. A General Introduction to Psychoanalysis. Wordsworth Editions, 2012.

Freud, Sigmund. The Ego and the Id. TACD Journal, 1989.

Holtz, Lou. Winning Every Day. Harper Business, 1998.

Katzenbach, Jon R., and Douglas K. Smith. "The Discipline of Teams." Harvard Business Review, Mar.- April 1993.

Kotsis, Sandra V, and Kevin C Chung. "Application of the "see one, do one, teach one" concept in surgical training." Plastic and reconstructive surgery vol. 131,5 (2013): 1194-1201. doi:10.1097/PRS.0b013e318287a0b3

Lucius Annaeus Seneca, (4 B.C.-A.D. 65) Roman Stoic philosopher, statesman, dramatist, "Seneca the Younger"

Maslow, Abraham H. "Self-actualizing People: A Study of Psychological Health." Personality Symposium, 1950.

Maslow, Abraham. Motivation and Personality. Harpers Press, 1954.

Maxwell, John C. JohnMaxwell.com. https://www.johnmaxwell.com/start-your-journey/

McKay, Adam, et al. Talladega Nights: The Ballad of Ricky Bobby. Widescreen unrated edition.Culver City, California, Sony Pictures Home Entertainment, 2006.

Newman, Aubrey S. Follow Me II. Presidio Press, 1992.

Newman, Aubrey. Follow Me III: Lessons on the Art and Science of High Command. Presidio Press, 1999.

Pichère, Pierre, and Anne-Christine Cadiat. Maslow's Hierarchy of Needs. Lemaitre, 2015.

Psychology Today (2023). Compartmentalization. https://shorturl.at/aiC28

Scott, Tony. Top Gun. Paramount Pictures, 1986.

Teschner, Robert C. The Methodology of the Debrief. 2006. Military Fighter Operations.

Theodore Roosevelt. "The Man in the Arena: Citizenship in a Republic." 23 April 1910, Sorbonne, Paris, France. Speech.

Wood, William J. Leaders & Battles. Presidio Press, 1995.

Wood, William J. Leaders and Battles. Presidio Press, 1984.

ABOUT THE
AUTHORS

Robert "Cujo" Teschner, former Air Force Colonel and retired Air Force fighter pilot, is the national best-selling author of *Debrief to Win: How America's Top Guns Practice Accountable Leadership...and How You Can, Too!* and best-selling co-author of *Aiming Higher: A Journey Through Military Aviation Leadership*, the first in the Military Mentorship Mastermind series. He is a former F-15C Eagle instructor at the prestigious US Air Force Weapons School and a former F-22 Raptor fighter squadron commander. Now he is the Founder and CEO of VMax Group, a St Louis-based international training company. In this capacity, Cujo is a highly sought-after motivational keynote speaker and corporate trainer. His expertise in leading high-performance teams enables him to bring high-performance team training into businesses of all shapes and sizes, helping drive buy-in, engagement, and performance. Cujo and his wife, Diane, are blessed to be parents to five beautiful children.

WWW.VMAXGROUPLLC.COM

WWW.ROBERTTESCHNER.COM

Chris "Elroy" Stricklin, Air Force Colonel (retired), is the award-winning, national best-selling co-author of *Survivor's Obligation: Navigating an Intentional Life*, detailing his ongoing journey in life to survive and thrive through the trauma of an aircraft ejection as an Air Force Thunderbird and *Aiming Higher: A Journey Through Military Aviation Leadership*, the first in the Military Mentorship Mastermind series. He is a highly sought-after motivational keynote speaker and a combat-proven senior military leader, retiring after 23 years of service which culminated with CEO-level leadership of a 7,000-person strong, $7B worldwide organization. His unique leadership style and skill have afforded him roles as a partner in a leadership consulting firm with impact across multiple Fortune 500 businesses. He now serves as the founding president of a first-of-its kind talent development organization, with leadership presentations and publications before millions of business leaders. Chris lives in Chelsea, Alabama with his wife, Terri. They have been blessed with four amazing children.

WWW.CHRISSTRICKLIN.COM

Luke "PSYCH" Layman, Lieutenant Colonel, is a combat veteran and recipient of the single mission air medal and combat action medal earned as an A-10C fighter pilot. He is a serial entrepreneur and investor, having led multiple seven and eight-figure businesses and the highest-performing organizations in the United States Air Force. With over two decades of leadership experience, PSYCH travels the world delivering keynotes and coaching CEOs to drive high-performance and bottom-line growth in their companies. Luke is a father to two beautiful children and a husband to an amazing wife, Jenny. He and his family reside in Charleston, SC.

WWW.LUKELAYMAN.COM

Robert "Shark" Garland, Air Force Colonel (retired) is the Founder and CEO of The Inspiring Eagle Foundation and a 32-year veteran of the United States Air Force and Defense Industry. He holds a US Patent as co-inventor of a revolutionary aviation design and was one of the first pilots chosen from across the Air Force to lead the operational test for the F-22 Raptor fighter jet. As Commandant of the Air Force Weapons School, he was a CEO-level leader responsible for writing curriculum and training all graduate level instructors, including combat and support specialties, for America's air power force. Robert is an instructor at VMax Group and a national transformational keynote speaker and corporate instructor. He is a graduate of the Center for Creative Leadership and holds Master's degrees in Aeronautical Science and National Strategies. Robert, his wife Amy, and their children Haley and Weston, live on a ranch in Central Texas.

Brian "Stickit" Emme, Navy Captain (retired), is an F/A-18 flight instructor combat veteran of two wars. He was privileged to command the Strike Fighter Squadron FOURTEEN Tophatters responsible for over 230 people and 12 F/A-18E jets totaling more than $800M in assets. He continued his career as the Air Boss of the nuclear-powered aircraft carrier USS *Carl Vinson* where he was responsible for the environment to enable the safe and efficient flight operations of 78 aircraft and all launch and recovery equipment enabling all weather, day or night flight operations in support of national tasking. He has over 3,000 flight hours in the F/A-18A-F, 768 carrier arrested landings and 25 years of hands-on leadership experience in High-Reliability Organizations. Brian is an instructor at VMax Group and an internationally sought-after transformational keynote speaker and corporate instructor. He is a graduate of Villanova University's Lean Six Sigma Certificate Program as a Black Belt. Brian, his wife Lisa, and their children Jake and Isabel, live in San Diego, California.

Made in United States
Orlando, FL
05 May 2023

32826482R00096